The
GIRVAN & PORTPATRICK JUNCTION RAILWAY

by
C.E.J. Fryer

THE OAKWOOD PRESS

© Oakwood Press 1994 and C.E.J. Fryer
ISBN 0 85361 448 2

Typeset by Gem Publishing Company, Brightwell, Wallingford, Oxfordshire.
Printed by Alpha Print (Oxford) Ltd, Witney, Oxfordshire.

Acknowledgements

I am specially indebted to Mr R. Ross Cunningham of Portpatrick, whose
encyclopaedic knowledge of this railway over the last thirty years has
enabled me to bring my own knowledge up to date. Many of the illustrations
were taken by him.

I am also much indebted to Mrs Rosemary Green of Barrhill, who drove
me round the bend – in fact, several bends between Girvan and Chirmorie –
to take some photographs of the line as it is now.

Anyone writing about this line is bound to acknowledge the help given by
the late David L. Smith, who knew this line in steam days like the back of his
hand.

Finally I am grateful to the Scottish Record Office, Edinburgh, and to the
National Library of Scotland, for opportunities to research.

Published by
The OAKWOOD PRESS
P.O.Box 122, Headington, Oxford OX3 8LU

Contents

	Introduction	5
Chapter One	The Promotion and Building of the Line	7
Chapter Two	Setbacks and Misfortunes: 1877–1892	9
Chapter Three	Under Glasgow and South Western Management: 1892–1922	13
Chapter Four	Under LMS and BR Management: 1923–1965	17
Chapter Five	The Route Described	21
Chapter Six	Train Services and Passenger Accommodation: 1877–1965	31
Chapter Seven	Locomotives Used Between 1877 and 1922	36
Chapter Eight	Locomotives Used Between 1922 and 1966	39
Chapter Nine	Accidents and Mishaps	46
Chapter Ten	A Fireman's Memories	51
Chapter Eleven	The Line Since 1965	55
Appendix One	Principal Events on the Girvan & Portpatrick Junction Railway	61
Appendix Two	Selected Timetables	62
Appendix Three	Types and Classes of Steam Locomotives used between Girvan and Stranraer	71
	Index	72

Bibliography

B. Baxter, ed. D. Baxter	*British Locomotive Catalogue: Vol. 4.*
H.J. Campbell Cornwell	*Forty Years of Caledonian Locomotives: 1882–1922.*
Campbell Highet	*The Glasgow & South Western Railway.*
Campbell Highet	*Scottish Locomotive History: 1831–1923.*
David L. Smith	*Tales of the Glasgow & South Western Railway.*
David L. Smith	*Legends of the Glasgow & South Western Railway in LMS days.*
David L. Smith	*Locomotives of the Glasgow & South Western Railway.*
David L. Smith	*The Little Railways of South-west Scotland.*
Various issues	*The Railway Magazine.*

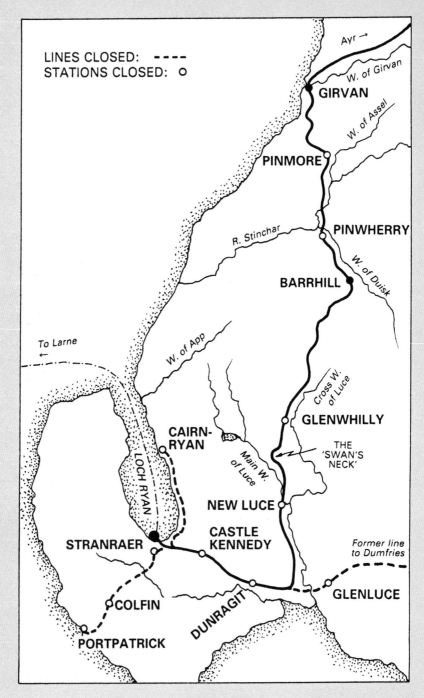

The Girvan and Portpatrick Junction Railway: 1965 and afterwards.

Introduction

Most railways built in the British Isles were constructed with some consideration for the services they could afford to intermediate places along their routes, and for the traffic that might be generated there. In regard to the line with which this book deals, such a consideration did not apply. Just as with an airline it is a matter of unconcern which places its aircraft fly over, so it scarcely mattered to the promoters of the Girvan and Portpatrick Junction Railway (G & PJR) which places it passed through. The main object was to complete a rail route to link Glasgow and Central Scotland directly, by way of the short sea crossing between Stranraer and Larne, with Ulster generally and Belfast in particular.

The alternative for most Glaswegians, once the Portpatrick Railway had been built but before the completion of the G & PJR, was to travel to Ulster either by way of Kilmarnock and Mauchline or Carstairs and Lockerbie to Dumfries and change there into a Stranraer-bound train, reaching that port only after a 155-mile journey from Glasgow – more if by way of Lockerbie. This route was so circuitous that it took less time to sail from Ardrossan all the way to Belfast than to take the short sea route with its attendant rail journey; in calm weather many preferred to do that and enjoy the scenic prospects *en route*, though the passage could be uncomfortable in winter for those who did not have sea legs. Once Girvan had been reached from Glasgow by rail in 1860, at the same time that the Portpatrick Railway's line from Castle Douglas to Stranraer was nearing completion, the 30-mile gap between Girvan and the nearest point on the latter cried out to be filled.

Two adverse factors hampered such a project. In the first place the terrain between Girvan and Stranraer presented difficulties; secondly the region was sparsely populated. However such a line might be routed, whether inland or along the coast, building it was bound to be costly; furthermore, it would take in no places of any size which would generate traffic locally. Consequently what would appear, from inspecting a map, to be a most desirable link in a rail-sea link between the largest Scottish city and the capital of Northern Ireland was not completed until 1877, by which time all the other main lines in Great Britain, with the single exception of the London extension of the Great Central Railway, had long been in operation. The G & PJR's promoters were not business men who wanted to invest their money in a promising scheme, but local people in Galloway and Carrick who, having pressed for the line to be built, supported it against all odds once it had been begun, unpromising though it sometimes seemed.

Having eventually been taken over by the Glasgow and South Western Railway (G & SWR), it became a main trunk route, though it remained single-tracked for nearly all its length, resembling in this respect the main lines of the Highland and Great North of Scotland Railways, from Perth to Inverness and from Aberdeen to Elgin. But even these lines could not match the severity of the G & PJR's steepest gradients, or display bleaker lineside scenery than that through which the latter passed as it traversed the barren uplands between the valleys of the river Stinchar and the Water of Luce. So the direct line from Glasgow to Stranraer, though it certainly saw brisk running, never had trains with fast timings. Heavy banks, and the need to exchange tokens at the passing loops, kept average speeds down, despite the fact that loads were usually light.

Inspection of a large-scale map of southern Scotland prompts the thought that the line need never have been built at all if some enterprising shipowner had realised the potential of Girvan itself as a cross-channel port. The distance thence to Larne is only a few miles further than from Stranraer. If a quay at Girvan could have been made suitable for ships of over 1,000 tons' burden at all states of the tide, and if the line, once built from Glasgow to Girvan, had been made to serve the harbour, a service could have been introduced similar to that from Stranraer. On the other hand, the port at Girvan is at a river mouth, where the making of a deep-water quay would have been a very expensive undertaking, and continual dredging would have been required. In addition, Girvan lacked the advantage provided at Stranraer of shelter from wind and wave because of the latter's position at the southern end of Loch Ryan. In fact the feasibility of Girvan being used as a passenger port does not seem to have occurred to anybody.

The railway came into existence by kind permission – or despite unkind opposition, for the mood varied – of the Portpatrick Railway, and managed through a trouble-fraught decade-and-a-half to keep going as an independent concern until taken over by the G&SWR. It was a vital link between Scotland and Northern Ireland during two World Wars, and suffered, in all, four changes of ownership. No one ever questioned its social utility, but in its later days it did not pay its way. When the Beeching Report of 1963 was published the inhabitants of south-west Scotland were aghast to discover that they stood to lose all their railways south of Ayr and west of Dumfries, and that there would no longer be any railway link to the Stranraer ferries. The consequent chorus of anger made British Railways think again, and the line from Ayr to Stranraer was spared, all rail services from all parts of England and Scotland to the short sea route being directed along it. Since that time there have been no further closures in this area, and although all the intermediate stations between Girvan and Stranraer except Barrhill have been closed, the through service is now quicker and in some respects better than ever before, and there are more ferry services now with which to connect. Long may this continue, but there are many cynics and pessimists who think that the road interests will win in the end, despite the fact that they are environmentally detrimental. Time will tell.

Chapter One
The Promotion and Building of the Line

When the Glasgow, Kilmarnock, Paisley and Ayr Railway (GKP&AR) reached the latter town in 1840 there was a call for it to be extended further south. The title given to the proposed scheme, the Glasgow and Belfast Union Railway (G&BUR), indicates what the proposers had in mind. It was to run by way of Girvan and Stranraer, following the coast between those places, and was to terminate at Portpatrick, whence at that time a packet service still plied to Donaghadee on the coast of County Down. There was no rail link then between Donaghadee and Belfast, but the Post Office shipped mails from the south of Scotland to Northern Ireland regularly by that route, and they were carried on to Belfast by road. Had the G&BUR ever been built, this no doubt would have been the manner in which passengers completed the journey. In fact no railway was constructed eastwards from Belfast in the direction of Donaghadee until May 1850, by which date the Post Office had ceased to use this route across the North Channel and was sending all mail by way of Holyhead and Kingstown.

The objective of the G&BUR was soon realised by its supporters not to be immediately obtainable, and they lowered their sights, pressing merely for a line as far as Girvan. An Act for the building of such a line was obtained from Parliament but never implemented. However, the scheme was resuscitated in 1853, though less ambitiously. The former GKP&AR had now, along with a number of other companies, been merged to form the Glasgow and South Western Railway, and the proposal was in the first instance to extend the line that had already reached Ayr as far as Maybole. Parliament authorised this in 1854 and the railway was opened to the latter town in 1856. Even before its completion its further extension to Girvan was also proposed and similarly authorised, and this second stage was completed in 1860.

Almost at once the possibility of its continuation southwards was canvassed. The Portpatrick Railway from Castle Douglas westwards was now being constructed, and the link from Girvan was envisaged as one that would join the other line either at Stranraer or to the east of it. The scheme was provisionally named the Girvan, Stranraer and North of Ireland Railway. Two possible routes were considered. One was to follow the coast through Ballantrae; the other would take a course more to the east, climbing southwards out of Girvan to a summit between the Bynehill Burn and the Water of Assel, descending into the valley of the Stinchar, rising again along the south-western side of the Duisk valley to a point just beyond Barrhill, turning south-west to cross the moors and then heading southwards to effect a junction with the Portpatrick Railway east of Stranraer. This would be more lengthy than the coastal route, but despite the need for a tunnel and several large bridges it would not work out as expensive as a route along the coast, where much rock would need to be blasted away.

A prospectus was issued in 1862 in which the inland route was specified. The scheme then hung fire for three years, during which period it was given a change of title. When the Act of Parliament authorising its construction was passed in July 1865 it had become simply the Girvan and Portpatrick Junction Railway. It was to issue £10 shares to a total of £250,000; in addition, up to £83,000 might be borrowed. One may compare this sum with that allowed for building the Portpatrick Railway (PR): £460,000 with extra powers to borrow up to £150,000. In that case the amount proved sufficient for just over 60 route miles of line. It was to be otherwise with the smaller company.

Again there was a delay, for people were reluctant to purchase shares. Eventually the time allowed for the line's construction ran out, and in June 1870 a further Act extended the time. Not until 1872 did the work actually begin. The contractor, Abraham Pilling of Bolton, Lancashire, obligingly agreed to take part of the company's stock of shares in payment, a decision he was later to regret. In 1872, also, permission was gained for running powers over the section of the Portpatrick Railway from Challoch Junction to Stranraer Town and Stranraer Harbour, on the understanding that the G&PJR would assume joint ownership of this stretch with the PR, and pay interest yearly on the first cost of this section.

The building of the line began at its northern end. It did not start from the existing station at Girvan, but branched off to the left shortly before that terminus was reached, a new one-platform station being established adjacent to the main road from Girvan to Maybole. Constructional difficulties at once began with the need to excavate the cutting through the flank of Dow Hill, which was rather less than half a mile long and some 60 feet deep at its central point. The next major task was the boring of the Pinmore tunnel, over a quarter of a mile long. Then followed the making of two viaducts. Building went ahead slowly, but by the end of the summer of 1874 all but the second viaduct had been completed. Unfortunately the contractor had now run into financial difficulties and needed more money, since he could not sell the shares he had been given in payment for the work done so far.

The money was found, a further Act of Parliament authorising the issue of £65,000 worth of Preference Stock. By now the building of the line had also begun from the southern end and the two teams began to approach each other. During the summer of 1875 work proceeded rapidly. Then came calamity. A tremendous storm struck the whole Galloway area at the end of September. All along the projected route earthworks were destroyed, bridges damaged, and the newly-finished viaduct across the Stinchar valley near Pinwherry was completely swept away.

Undiscouraged, the promoters came to the aid of the contractor and provided him with three additional small locomotives to enable material to be moved. (The two which had previously been available to Pilling were now not enough, as the line had been breached in a number of places and work had to be done on five fronts instead of only two.) A contract was also placed with a Glasgow firm of engineers to replace the former stone bridge across the Stinchar by an iron one. By the end of 1876 the railway was virtually completed. It was (and still is) single-tracked all the way, with crossing loops at each of the five intermediate stations, each with a signal cabin; there was also a crossing loop at Challoch Junction, where it joined the Portpatrick Railway.

On 24th July, 1877 the Board of Trade inspection took place, the Inspector, General Hutchinson traversing the whole line in a train supplied by the G&SWR. The full public service began on 5th October, 1877. The line's building had been beset with difficulties, but now, it was thought, Fortune would at last smile and profits accrue. It was to be a vain hope.

Chapter Two
Setbacks and Misfortunes: 1877–1892

As already indicated, the new line was bound to some extent to compete with the Portpatrick Railway since it provided a shorter and quicker rail route between Glasgow and Stranraer. The prospect of its being built at all had seemed at first rather remote, but the PR's Directors kept a steady eye on what went on, and after the Act of 1865 which authorised its construction had been passed they had to come to terms with reality. It was some comfort that the line was not going to take the coastal route through Ballantrae but was instead aiming to join their own metals at Challoch Junction, since the use of their own line thence to Stranraer would bring them a little revenue to offset the losses from the sale of tickets from Glasgow via Dumfries. As three members of the PR Board were also Directors of the G&PJR the attitude of each towards the other was bound to be to some extent ambivalent, but in general the PR's Directors were not friendly to the new venture.

Once construction of the G&PJR had begun, the PR was at first ready to accept the inevitable with a good grace, but then came the knowledge that the former's Board was considering building a separate line from Challoch to Stranraer. Relations at once became soured, for if this were to happen the revenue the PR counted on receiving would not come its way. In fact this line was never constructed, but the animosity lingered. The Provost of Stranraer, who had supported the building of the new line, though he was also a PR Director, stood up for the rights of the former at Board meetings, and the debates there were sometimes acrimonious.

Once the line from Girvan had been finished it was necessary for the two companies to agree over what sums the G&PJR should pay the PR, both annually for the use of the tracks, stations and East Pier at Stranraer, and also in a single payment towards the costs of the facilities that the PR had originally had to provide. As the two parties could not come to a mutually acceptable settlement the matter went to arbitration early in 1878, and the distinguished civil engineer, Sir Thomas Bouch, to whom the dispute was referred, took two years to come to a decision. (He was much distracted during this time, since the first Tay Bridge, designed by him, collapsed in a storm during January 1879, taking a train-load of people to their deaths.) He made his award in June 1880, spelt out to the nearest farthing. It amounted to a sum not far short of £10,000, payable there and then, plus half the annual costs of using and maintaining the pier, whatever these might be. It was up to the G&PJR to meet this debt as quickly as it could.

However, difficulties at once began to arise. The company had contracted with the G&SWR for the latter to work the line in return for nine-tenths of the gross receipts. There was not enough left over during the period when this agreement was in force to pay any of the money due to the PR, and the interest on the debt thus incurred began to mount. Other debts, too, were outstanding, and when it became clear that these also could not be met immediately the creditors petitioned for the company to be taken over by a Judicial Factor. In July 1879 this was done, an Edinburgh chartered accountant, James Haldane, being appointed by the Court of Session to manage the company and, if possible, put straight its financial affairs.

Haldane faced a very difficult position. His task was eased a little by an agreement, made some while previously with the G&SWR, to make a more realistic charge for working the line, but although the cost of locomotive provision fell during the next six months, that of maintenance increased. On 31st January, 1881 Haldane told the G&SWR that he intended to terminate the second agreement. The shareholders questioned his right to do this, but a Court judgement upheld him. He later obtained the shareholders' agreement to selling the line if a buyer could be found. The G&SWR, who had certainly not wanted the line to close, or to lose any influence they had over its operation, agreed to continue to work it on a month-to-month basis. It is worth here considering the viewpoints of all the parties. The G&PJR Board and shareholders wished the line to continue to operate, preferably under their control, but if not, at least with the burden of debt being removed. The G&SWR also wanted the line to continue working, and would have liked to get control of it if they could have done so at small expense to themselves. The PR would no doubt have preferred the line to have closed down entirely but realised that, with so much capital having been sunk in it, this was unlikely to happen. What they chiefly wished was for the debts due to themselves to be settled, and these were mounting month by month. Haldane, acting for the debtors generally, was not interested in whether the line went on operating, but only in securing the best possible results for his clients.

In January 1882 he approached the G&PJR shareholders and persuaded them to agree to the promotion of a Parliamentary Bill to raise £50,000 in fresh stock, so that the debts owed to existing creditors could be met and locomotives and rolling stock might be purchased to operate the line independently. This was bound to take time, and it was anybody's guess whether the needed money could all be raised in this way. The PR Board decided that it could wait no longer, and in February 1882 closed the line between Challoch Junction and Stranraer to the trains of the G&PJR. All they actually gained by doing this was a small reduction in working expenses. The Caledonian Railway (CR), which then worked the PR, no doubt relished the chance of doing its competitors, the G&SWR, a bad turn; in any case, this denial of facilities was bound to tighten the screw on the G&PJR a little further.

In the event Parliament granted the promoters' request and the Bill became an Act, though the power to raise £50,000 was modified, the permitted maximum being £30,000. The G&SWR now agreed to work the G&PJR on more moderate terms, and in addition purchased £20,000 worth of the new stock and promised to pay a fixed amount annually to the PR towards the eventual settlement of its claim. They also agreed to work the line on the basis of retaining a proportion of the gross receipts on a sliding scale varying from 75 per cent to 55 per cent, according to whether they were low or high. Any money left over would go to the G&PJR's shareholders. Thus the matter appeared to be settled to everyone's satisfaction for the two years during which the agreement was to operate, which ended in September 1885.

For a short while it looked as if the Girvan line's troubles were over. Trains ran once more between New Luce and Stranraer. After a year's operation the company even managed to declare a dividend of 1 per cent. But elsewhere events were brewing which brought the brief interlude of prosperity to a close. The Portpatrick Railway's days of independence, by its own wish, were numbered. In 1864 it had made a very advantageous agreement with the CR for working its line, and it was known that the latter were going to demand much stiffer terms in 1885. So various wheels had been set turning, and the end result was that a Joint Board of both the Portpatrick and Wigtownshire Railways was established, and the operation of its services west of Castle Douglas, including the branch from Newton Stewart to Whithorn, was undertaken jointly by the CR and G&SWR, each contributing locomotives and rolling stock, and each alternating in the general management of the line, three years at a time. The Board itself included representatives from both the constituent railways, and. also of the Midland and London and North Western companies in England. Thus after August 1885 the G&SWR was involved at the Stranraer end of the line as well as at Girvan itself. It gave notice that it would terminate the existing agreement with the G&PJR six months later.

The latter's Directors shrewdly suspected what the G&SWR was up to. Since there was no Parliamentary sanction for selling the line to the highest bidder it was no doubt hoping that a closure would be forced and that the South Western company could then obtain it for a knock-down price. The Directors at once mounted a counter-offensive and drafted yet another Parliamentary Bill asking:

(1) for running powers over the G&SWR from Girvan to Kilwinning and Kilmarnock (to both of which places the CR had its own lines) so that a service from the CR terminus at Glasgow to Stranraer might be possible)
(2) the enlargement of the single-platform station at Girvan to deal with goods traffic
(3) the borrowing of up to £25,000 to enable them to work the line themselves
(4) a provision that the power of selling the line should rest solely with its own directors.

At the same time they decided to appoint a General Manager, and W.J. Wheatley, the son of Thomas Wheatley, a former locomotive superintendent of the North British Railway who had latterly managed the Wigtownshire Railway, was asked to take the post. He agreed, giving up a well-paid position as locomotive foreman at Stranraer for the Portpatrick and Wigtownshire Joint Committee in return for the more prestigious, but financially riskier position, on the Girvan line. The latter for a while now became completely independent. It hired rolling stock from the G&SWR as well as purchasing locomotives, wagons and carriages, and appointed its own staff, after the Parliamentary Bill had become an Act in April 1886.

Once more the fortunes of the G&PJR appeared to be on the mend – though those in authority on the G&SWR no doubt hoped and expected that the better times would not last long and that they would eventually be able to scoop up a bankrupt concern. Their prey did not fall to them so quickly. In May 1887 a consortium of London business men offered to purchase the line, and the G&PJR shareholders agreed – though they must have reflected that the buyers were getting a bargain, since for £166,500 a railway was being bought which had cost more than three times that sum to build. On 1st August, 1887 it passed to its new owners and its name was changed to the Ayrshire and Wigtownshire Railway (A&WR).

From 1888 to 1891 the company, under the new regime, managed to pay its way and have enough left over to give a small dividend to the shareholders and also buy a little new equipment. Thanks to the hard work and enterprise of W.J. Wheatley and his staff the line kept its head above water financially. But it was not a money-spinner. It generated no local traffic worth mentioning, and competing steamer services from Ardrossan to Belfast charging low fares attracted people away from the short sea route. Meanwhile much of the rolling stock was wearing out – in particular the second-hand engines that Wheatley had obtained. The next-to-last incident in the G&PJR's chequered history was its sale to one of the members of its Board. The buyers of 1887 had been anxious to make money rather than to ensure the continuance of the train service and they had no sentimental attachment to the A&W's fortunes. When it became evident that the line was not likely to become a source of profit the Directors were willing enough to sell out to one of their number, an Edinburgh lawyer, John Blair, who had the ready money but merely wanted to sell the railway and make a profit for himself.

Blair did his best but could not find a purchaser. Meanwhile the plant and rolling stock were deteriorating. Unserviceable locomotives were cannibalised to provide parts for repairing others, and in 1891 there were only five locomotives left. Finally Wheatley, whose energies and expertise had been freely expended in the vain hope of making ends meet, lost heart and resigned his position as Manager; he bought a Stranraer hotel and concluded an eventful railway career by catering for tourists, at which he was very successful.

For fifteen years the winds had blown fair and foul; now the whirlwind moved in to devour its prey. The moment the G&SWR had been waiting for had now arrived. In February 1892 it bought the A&WR after an Act of Parliament had authorised it to do so on condition that the line be put into proper repair. The price paid was £270,000, less than half the original cost of construction; however, a good deal had to be spent in renovating the cuttings, tunnel, bridges and viaducts and relaying the track with heavier rails and better ballast. Much of the rolling stock was disposed of for scrap, and the staff found that their salaries and wages were reduced. But at least the line's future from then on was secure. It made sense for the railway company which dominated the south-west of Scotland to control the whole line and integrate its services with theirs. For the next 30 years the G&SWR was to do this, and under its ownership services improved.

Chapter Three
Under Glasgow and South Western Management: 1892–1922

When a small railway gives up the struggle for independence and is obliged to be absorbed into a larger concern a certain amount of regret is natural, but it is often in the best interests of those who use it that this should happen. The low price that the G&SWR paid when it bought the A&WR was partly because the fixed plant, locomotives and rolling stock were in a deplorable state, and the new owners at once set in hand the necessary improvements, following reports from their locomotive superintendent, James Manson, and their Chief Engineer, William Melville. The latter's report especially emphasised the condition that the railway had been allowed to get into during the vicissitudes of the previous 15 years. Most of the existing lineside fencing was thoroughly dilapidated, and the same was the case with the interiors of houses that had been built for the staff. The ballast beneath the track was generally unsatisfactory, as also were most of the sleepers. The rails were not stout enough to take the traffic safely. All the points and crossings needed renewing. Pinmore tunnel would have to be largely re-lined. The stonework of the viaducts needed re-pointing. All the wayside stations needed to be overhauled. In some bridges the timbers needed replacement, and the viaduct across the Stinchar required a second repair since the first one had not been done properly.

As to the locomotives and rolling stock, the tank engines that had been bought second-hand when the line was built were now, Manson reckoned, only fit for scrapping. The four 0–6–0 tender locomotives more recently built were still serviceable, although three needed to be repaired. The passenger carriages were in a bad state; 14 had worn-out wheels and had been kept standing idle in consequence; only six recently-built ones were fit to be used. Four milk vans, three horse-boxes and a carriage truck, originally obtained second-hand, were unusable because of the state of their wheels and springs. Ten goods vans and ten goods wagons, recently built, were serviceable; of the four goods brake vans two were relatively new and could still be used; the rest were only fit for scrapping. Twenty-five cattle wagons, bought second-hand, had not seen much use, and with modifications to their buffing gear could be made serviceable for employment between Girvan and Stranraer, though not elsewhere.

The recommended alterations and reconstructions to the line and its structures were begun at once and quickly carried through, though the re-lining of the tunnel (which had been partly lined with metal plates when first built) took time to complete. New rails, 90 lb. to the yard, were laid throughout on creosoted sleepers set in stone ballast. The staff houses were re-conditioned with fresh plaster on the interior walls. At Girvan, where there had been two passenger stations, the original terminus and the single platform built by the G&PJR, the latter was retained and rebuilt with two platforms, while the former was demolished, only the goods station being kept. Many of the cuttings, which were too steeply-angled for safety, were widened to give gentler slopes. New frames were installed in the signal boxes, and the electric tablet system was installed. The wayside stations were all refurbished.

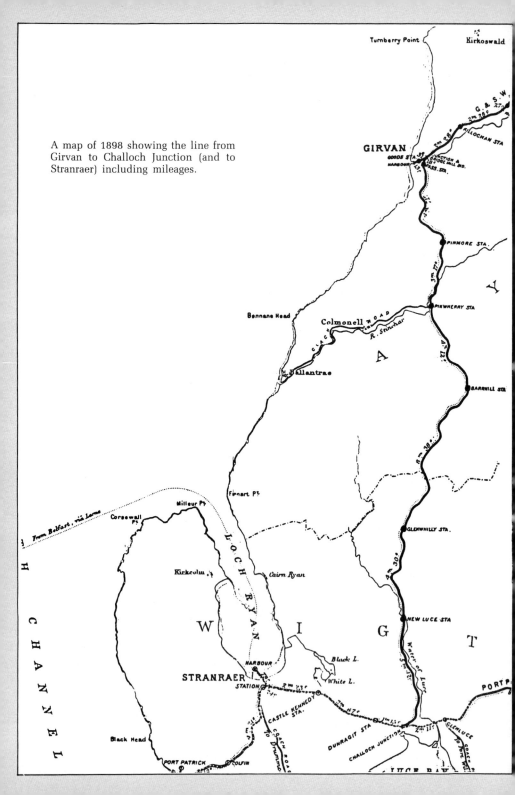

A map of 1898 showing the line from Girvan to Challoch Junction (and to Stranraer) including mileages.

Improvements in the train services followed, as can be seen from a comparison of the timetables. In 1891 under A & WR management the early morning, mid-morning, afternoon and evening southbound trains all took between 90 and 95 minutes from Girvan to Stranraer, stopping at all stations, and it was much the same in the opposite direction except that the evening boat express, omitting most stops, reached Girvan in 75 minutes from Stranraer Harbour. In 1893, on the other hand, the down timings of the all-stations trains had quickened to between 83 and 89 minutes, with a 66-minute timing for the down boat express. Northbound, the corresponding timings were between 85 and 87 minutes for the stopping trains and a fast 62 minutes for the train connecting with the evening boat from Larne. Between Glasgow and Stranraer the shortest time came down from 3½ hours to 2 hours 55 minutes, and in the other direction from 4 hours to 2 hours 52 minutes.

This was a definite advance, and in regard to one particular train there was later to be a really startling acceleration. After the G & SWR had in 1899 introduced a 3-coach train of bogie corridor stock for the boat services, the schedules were cut still further, and in 1904 the 'Paddy', as the evening up boat express was colloquially termed, had its Girvan stop removed and was timed to run from Stranraer Harbour to Ayr in 83 minutes. Such a timing for 59 miles, had the load not been under 100 tons, would have been impossible, considering the small engines that were used, and over a line so severely graded, on which there was also the need to slow down several times to exchange tablets at passing loops. However, the footplate crews rose to the challenge. David L. Smith's comments, in his book about the railways of south-west Scotland, are worth quotation.

> Running then became truly fast and furious. It was a test of endurance, both for men and for engines – the grades, the severe curves, and above all the sharp turn-outs of the crossing loops. Firemen reached Ayr at night with arms black and blue from the catching of tablets as they rocked and tore through those awful loops. Then, one day in 1906, all drivers in the 'Paddy' link were called into the office at Ayr sheds and had read to them a letter from James Manson giving warning that unless they mended their ways there would be 'another Salisbury disaster.'* Nevertheless it was 1911 before the schedule was altered, the time from leaving Stranraer Harbour to passing Girvan being increased from a furious 55 to a sober 63 minutes. Another deterrent was the introduction in 1910 of an apparatus for the exchange of tablets devised by Mr William Bryson, the G & SWR signal engineer, for in its original form it was incapable of exchanging at much over 30 miles an hour.†

One wonders which was the more effective deterrent, Manson's warning, or Bryson's railway equivalent of a 'sleeping policeman'. However, in all the 30 years of G & SWR ownership of the Girvan to Stranraer line there were no accidents to passenger trains, though there were some to goods trains. As to the faster schedules, it would seem that they encouraged traffic, and especially holiday traffic. The lure of the Ardrossan to Belfast steamer service

---

*Early in the morning of 1st July, 1906 the special night express carrying passengers from Plymouth who had disembarked from a transatlantic liner took the curve through Salisbury station at an excessive speed and was derailed. Twenty-eight people lost their lives, including the driver and fireman. No explanation was ever found for the driver's disregard for the speed restriction, but it appeared that this train often travelled too fast through Salisbury without mishap, and the belief may have arisen that the 30-mph restriction was un-necessarily cautious.
†D.L. Smith: The Little Railways of South West Scotland: pp. 171–172.

became less tempting as the quality of the ride to Stranraer improved and corridor coaches made possible the satisfaction of certain basic needs while travelling, which previously only the steamship could provide.

The advent of World War I necessarily brought about a worsening of the service. The daytime boat trains were withdrawn at the beginning of 1915 and the evening one two years later. However, in 1916 the Easter Rising in Dublin heralded a long period of active Nationalist discontent and it was considered necessary to station British troops in Ireland. A regular un-timetabled daily train was then put on in either direction between Glasgow and Stranraer to cater for those going on or off leave. There were also special coal trains which transported fuel for the naval patrol vessels and mine-sweepers. But, as was the case all over the country, maintenance suffered through shortage of staff during 1914–1918, so that the state of the line deteriorated; consequently, even when peace returned there could be no immediate restoration of the fast running of pre-war years. Travel to or from Stranraer was by stopping trains which did not make prompt connections with the boats to and from Larne, so that one might have to wait for up to three hours before crossing. Indeed, in 1922 the rail service was poorer than it had been 30 years earlier. Improvements had to wait until after the G & SWR had been merged into the London Midland and Scottish Railway.

153.—GIRVAN AND PORTPATRICK JUNCTION.

Incorporated by 28 and 29 Vic., cap. 358 (5th July, 1865), to construct a line from Girvan, on the Maybole, to a junction with the Portpatrick, at East Challock. Length, 30¾ miles. Capital, 250,000*l.* in shares, and 83,300*l.* on loan. Works not commenced.

No. of Directors—6 ; minimum, 4 ; quorum, 3. *Qualification*, 500*l.*

DIRECTORS:

Chairman—DAVID GUTHRIE, Esq., Stranraer.

Colonel Macdowall, of Logan.	David Frederick, Esq., Dumbreddan, by
Sir J. C. D. Hay, Bart., M.P., of Park Place,	Stranraer.
108, St. George's Square, S.W.	

OFFICERS.—Auditors, J. Graham and W. Murray : Solicitors, H. and R. Lamond, Glasgow, and Millar, Allardice, and Robson, Edinburgh.

Offices—Stranraer, and 64, West Regent Street, Glasgow.

Extract from the 1872 *Bradshaw's Shareholders Manual.*

A 1906 view of George Street, Stranraer as depicted on an early postcard published by Valentines.   *Oakwood Collection*

The beach as seen from the pier at Girvan in 1935.   *Oakwood Collection*

The village street in Barrhill showing typical lowland Scottish house styles.

Author's Collection

The village of Barrhill, seen from near the railway station, with the Merrick and other summits of the Galloway Hills on the horizon, to the east.   *Author's Collection*

The remains of the former Cistercian Abbey near New Luce, about half a mile from the railway station. *Author's Collection*

The cloisters of the Abbey at New Luce. *Author's Collection*

Part of the eleven-arch viaduct, photographed in May 1992, which crossed the tributary-burn of the Water of Assel, between Pinmore and Pinwherry. Note the reinforcement of the piers with iron bands.   *Author*

A fine view of Pinmore Viaduct from the train, looking south in July 1957.
H.C. Casserley

An early view of Pinwherry station showing the acute curves of this section of line and the platform waiting shelter built on wooden supports.   *Lens of Sutton*

The site of Pinwherry station as seen in May 1992, just after the removal of the passing loop.   *Author*

Glendoune cutting, looking north, photographed in May 1992 from the overbridge. In the days of steam, leaf falls could bring the trains to a stand here!   *Author*

The staggered platforms of New Luce station, looking north-east. Taken in the 1900s, it shows a domeless Stirling 4−4−0 entering with a passenger service. *Lens of Sutton*

'Black Five' No. 45687 and Standard class '5' No. 73079 double-head a train for Stranraer in July 1957, near the summit between Barrhill and Glenwhilly.

H.C. Casserley

Pinwherry station looking north in July, 1957. The train is the 11.40 am from Stranraer, headed by 'Black Five' No. 45728.

H.C. Casserley

Dunragit station buildings. These are now closed but the crossing gates were still in use in October 1969, when this photograph was taken. *Ross Cunningham*

Underline bridge near milepost 16, photographed in May 1992, with steps giving access to the running line for permanent way staff. *Author*

Chapter Four

Under LMS and BR Management: 1923–1965

With the formation of the London Midland and Scottish Railway the centre for policy direction on Scottish lines moved to London. Here, though the needs of the whole system were doubtless impartially considered, the local interests of particular areas no longer mattered so much. One unfortunate consequence of this change was the almost total destruction of all former G&SWR locomotives still existing in 1923 which took place between then and 1939. Another consequence was the disappearance of the former bitter rivalry between the G&SWR and the CR, which was followed by a tendency for these systems' former employees to unite in opposition to proposals emanating from their new masters south of the Border. It was to be a long while before the LMS became internally unified and got its act together.

One of the first things to happen after the amalgamation was an economy campaign, showing itself in small measures aimed at reducing expenses, taking care of the pence so that the pounds could take care of themselves. An example of this was the lengthening of block sections on single lines to reduce the number of manned signal boxes. On the former G&PJR route proper the effect was small – merely that Pinmore box was switched out of operation except for a short period each day. Between Challoch Junction and Stranraer, on the other hand, not only was the whole of this section made into a single block, the points at Challoch being electrically worked from Dunragit, but the previous system of automatic tablet exchange devised by James Manson was done away with, since so many locomotives would now need the exchange device to be fitted if that practice were to continue that the cost would have been excessive. So recourse was again had to hand exchange along the whole of the former Portpatrick Railway. In theory this required the locomotives to slow down very considerably at the passing loops; in practice they were taken faster than intended. West of Challoch Junction, therefore, the firemen on the Girvan to Stranraer run became adept at hooking the loop of the tablet holder over their left arm, wearing jackets specially reinforced with leather, or padded in some way, so that they did not injure themselves.

A problem which began to show itself during the 1920s, and became more evident during the 1930s was that, as trains became longer, the passing loops became less and less able to accommodate them when one had to be crossed with another. At Pinmore and Glenwhilly this could not be done with passenger trains of the minimum length now customary. Barrhill could just manage two trains of eight coaches, Pinwherry and New Luce two of nine coaches. If loads went beyond these limits it became necessary to do some shunting into and out of sidings, and long delays could result. The first sign of improvement came in 1937, when a second platform was built at Glenwhilly, which was about half-way between Girvan and Stranraer, and the loops were extended to take double-headed 12-coach trains if necessary. This mitigated the problem but did not entirely solve it. Later, during World War II, when a more intensive use of the line became a necessity, what had been done to the loop at Glenwhilly had also to be done at the other stations.

During the 1930s the line prospered as never before or since. Not only were more and longer trains despatched along it on weekdays, but during the summer months Sunday excursions disturbed the hitherto-customary sabbath calm. There is much photographic evidence from this time of long, double-headed passenger trains. During the 1920s and 1930s the private car was a luxury affordable only by families that were comfortably well off; its use had not yet spread to the lower income groups. Coach and bus services were increasing in number and frequency, but their threat to the railways' financial prosperity was as yet potential rather than actual. This period was the line's heyday, when restaurant cars ran through from Glasgow to Stranraer, as they had not done before and were never to do again. The outbreak of World War II rudely ended this prosperity.

Two things then happened to alter the pattern of passenger patronage. The public as a whole was urged not to travel by rail unless it had to. 'Is your journey really necessary?' faced people on posters in station forecourts. In addition the placing of troops in Ulster meant that numbers of them were all the time going on or off leave. The use of the lines leading to Stranraer therefore declined so far as civilians were concerned, while travel by service personnel increased greatly between 1939 and 1945. At the same time fewer trains were run, and this made journeys more crowded and less comfortable. In addition, despite slower schedules timekeeping deteriorated.

One event, which might have overloaded the line if the course of the war had gone as some had anticipated, was the establishment of a temporary port at Cairnryan, some distance north of Stranraer along the east shore of Loch Ryan. It was believed in governmental circles that the enemy would try to put either Glasgow or Liverpool out of action through air bombardment, so this new port was constructed as a substitute, where ocean-going vessels could load and unload at deep-water quays. These were sited along both sides of a long pier which extended southwards from Cairnryan Point and was well provided with cranes. A single-track railway was also built to link the existing line at Stranraer with the port. It diverged from the main line a mile short of the town, ran alongside it for a few hundred yards, then curved sharply to the north, following the shore close to the A77 coastal road to Girvan and Glasgow. Two and a half miles short of the port itself there were extensive sidings with room for 2,000 wagons; there were also two smaller marshalling yards, one beside the junction near the town and the other a mile north of the main yard. The port had accommodation for several ocean-going ships on either side of the main pier.

The construction of Cairnryan harbour began in January 1941 and continued for two and a half years. It was built by members of the Armed Forces, many of whom were USA citizens who had to wear civilian clothing until the USA entered the war after the Japanese attack on Pearl Harbour. Once completed, it was worked entirely by the Ministry of Defence. Locomotives bringing freight trains or taking them away were not allowed to pass more than a few hundred yards along the branch; Ministry of Defence engines then took over. How useful Cairnryan might have been had Glasgow or Liverpool been put out of action one cannot tell, but its potential was never realised. Only 18 fully-loaded ocean-going vessels discharged there during the war years. However, it was also used for landing goods from Ulster – notably large quantities of milk. The approach line was also used to carry workers to the port from the outskirts of Stranraer, and some superannuated six-wheeled carriages which had once belonged to the L&NWR together with a few ancient L&YR eight-wheelers performed this duty. They and the wagon-trains that carried goods inland from the port were worked by 0–6–0 tank engines borrowed from the GWR and LNER.

Once the war was over Cairnryan harbour was not needed, but before being dismantled it was used to load redundant gas shells on to ships for dumping in mid-Atlantic. The shells were conveyed from the depots where they had been stored by special freight trains. On one occasion an accident that could have been very nasty indeed was averted through the quick action of a railway signalman. A coupling snapped on one of these trains as it was climbing Glendoune Bank, and the rear portion, made up of 18 wagons loaded with gas shells, together with the guard's van, in which the brake was not strong enough to hold it stationary on the incline, rushed back downwards to Girvan station. Fortunately it did not collide with another train which was already standing at the station, as the points had been set to protect the latter, but it went right through on a clear line and eventually came to a stand. Had there been a collision the consequences for the town of Girvan could have been truly appalling.

Once the gas shells had all been disposed of, Cairnryan became for a time a shipbreaker's yard and several vessels were broken up there, including World War I Dreadnought HMS *Ramillies*. The War Department finally vacated the place in 1959 and the port and its equipment were sold to a contractor. It has not been used since, though a mile to the south a quay was later built near Cairnryan village from which a vehicle ferry now plies to Larne in competition with the boats from Stranraer. The linking railway was dismantled at the end of 1962.

The exigencies of the war obliged the LMS to make other changes. It was doubtful whether the existing single line between Challoch Junction and Stranraer could possibly have coped with the expected traffic from Cairnryan if that port had been brought into full operation, so it was decided to double this section of the railway. However, in the event only the part between Dunragit and Castle Kennedy was doubled, and this in effect became a passing loop three miles long. At about the same time the other station passing loops at New Luce, Barrhill, Pinwherry and Pinmore were also lengthened to match the arrangement at Glenwhilly, and long-bladed points were installed at the junction so that non-stopping trains could go through at up to 50 mph. Between Challoch Junction and Girvan the Bryson tablet-catching apparatus, now improved to cope with higher speeds, was already in use to facilitate this. At Dunragit and Castle Kennedy, however, hand exchange was now again the practice; this section, too, was accordingly Bryson-fitted. The Bryson apparatus had the great advantage of being easily fixable and detachable; unlike the Manson apparatus it could be fitted to any locomotive quickly and cheaply. So, for a while, automatic tablet exchange was the rule along the whole Girvan–Stranraer line.

During the war years the Stranraer–Larne ferry service carried more than five million passengers, Armed Forces personnel outnumbering civilians by more than six times. Extra ships had to be called in to make additional crossings. As for the connecting train services, the strain on the rolling stock was considerable but the latter, though overworked and poorly maintained, managed to keep going. The closure of Girvan engine shed in 1941 was a hindrance to smooth operation. Once hostilities were over recovery was slow, and the former readiness of the travelling public to use the train had disappeared; they went by bus instead when they could. Train services, such as the mid-day up and afternoon down boat trains and the late evening service from Glasgow, came back, but patronage was poor. The ships plying between Stranraer and Larne were now beginning to take private cars, so motorists could drive direct to the port and embark there. Direct air services, too, were beginning to operate between Glasgow and Belfast. So the final days of LMS ownership were sad and unprofitable.

When in 1948 British Railways took over the lines in south-west Scotland it was inevitable that there would be some closures. The branches from Stranraer to Portpatrick and from Newton Stewart to Whithorn had long ceased to pay their way, and in 1950 both were closed to passengers. The former G&PJR, however, though a single-track line, was part of a trunk route, and remained open, the pattern of train services remaining much as before. New steam motive power appeared, as related in a later chapter. In 1959 a change was made in regard to the passenger services, when diesel multiple units replaced steam-hauled trains. Some were provided with buffet facilities, which had eventually to be withdrawn from lack of patronage. Freight trains continued to be locomotive-hauled. The introduction of the multiple unit diesel trains would, it was first thought, pose a problem, that of exchanging tablets; there were now no firemen who could see to this. Drivers found in practice that they could catch the lightly-made hoops attached to the tablet bags by lowering their side windows and hooking them up with their left arms, so long as the speed was 30 mph or less. This practice was winked at for a while, but considerable dexterity was needed, and authority eventually decided that it should cease, and an instruction was issued that every train had to stop while the tablets were exchanged. The tablet catchers and holders on the station platforms were now no longer needed and were dismantled.

Over the years there had been many changes to the lines in south-west Scotland. In 1965 something like a death sentence was threatened. Dr Richard Beeching had been appointed as Chairman of the British Transport Commission, with a mandate for sweeping changes to improve the railways' financial viability. What happened under his *aegis* is related in the final chapter.

Chapter Five
The Route Described

The actual distance between Girvan North Junction and Challoch Junction, the northern and southern limits of the original line as built in 1877, was just short of 31 miles, Stranraer Town station being between 6 and 7 miles further on along the former Portpatrick Railway's metals, and the Harbour station about ½ mile further still. For sheer difficulty no other main line in the United Kingdom can match this stretch, except perhaps the final 30 miles of the former GWR line from London to Plymouth, which indeed has parts more steeply graded, but these are shorter than those between Girvan and Stranraer. Even the main line of the former Highland Railway, which at two places reaches an altitude twice as high above sea level as the G&PJR's summit at Chirmorie, has no gradient steeper than 1 in 60, whereas the stretch now under consideration has 6½ miles more steeply inclined even than that.

The G&PJR began just short of the former terminus of the Ayr and Girvan Railway, which was sited close to the loop of the Girvan Water just before this stream curved round to pass the harbour and enter the Firth of Clyde. Swinging to the left, the line for Stranraer crosses the latter stream and the main road from Girvan to Ayr, and enters Girvan station. Originally there was only a single platform here, but the G&SWR rebuilt it with two and there has been further reconstruction since. The present station comprises a single platform for northbound trains (sometimes used for southbound trains as well), adjacent to which are the entrance from the above-mentioned road and the usual station offices. At the other side of an under-pass is an island platform from whose two faces southbound trains departed formerly, but at present only the inner face is used. The present station buildings are comparatively new, and are in concrete and red brick; there are also some sidings. The former terminus became a goods depot; this has now vanished, the rails have been lifted and houses are being built on the site.

Immediately beyond the platform ends – indeed, right at the spot where the locomotives used to refill their tanks from the water-column – begins one of the line's two fiercest banks, a hundred yards or so at 1 in 50, 2½ miles at 1 in 54, followed after a few yards at 1 in 50 by a mile at 1 in 56. This stretch, which present-day Super Sprinter units manage without difficulty, faced engines in the days of steam with a dreadful task, particularly as part of it, Glendoune cutting, was liable to become leaf-strewn in the autumn and adhesion might be reduced to zero.

The line appears at first to be making for the ridge of high grassy hills which shut Girvan in to the south-east, but it then veers round, first to the south, then to the south-west, passing through the deep Glendoune cutting by which it circumvents the rounded eminence of Dow Hill and its Iron Age earthworks. After emerging from the cutting it traverses an embankment from which a splendid backward view of the Clyde estuary becomes visible for a few seconds, affording glimpses of the mountains of Arran and the Isle of Bute. The main A714 road from Girvan to Newton Stewart now approaches the line from the right, and after curving into the valley of the Bynehill Burn the railway goes under it and keeps it in view to the left until the approach to Pinmore tunnel, over the top of which the road again crosses the line.

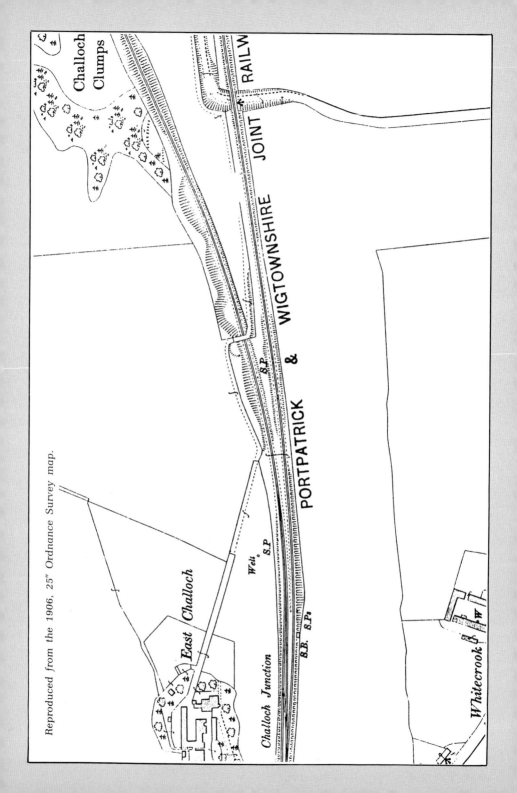

Reproduced from the 1906, 25" Ordnance Survey map.

Pinmore tunnel, a straight bore 543 yards long, is a little beyond the actual summit at milepost 4. The line now descends for 4½ miles on gradients that vary between 1 in 65 and 1 in 300. Just under a mile from the tunnel's southern exit was Pinmore station, which had a single platform, a crossing loop and a signal cabin; all were dismantled in 1964. One has now reached the valley of the Assel Water, and the descent continues along its right bank, crossing *en route* the Kinclaer viaduct which carries it across a tributary burn of the Assel and beneath which the A714 road loops right, and then left again at a much lower level. Soon after this one enters the wide valley of the Stinchar and crosses this stream by Lagansarroch viaduct. Its left bank is now followed until, at Pinwherry village, one reaches the foot of the descent and the site of what was formerly the chief intermediate station between Girvan and Stranraer. Now closed, it had two platforms, with a loop and a signal box, and was picturesquely situated close to the point where the Stinchar, joined by the Duisk, turns away to the west along a broadening valley. At Pinwherry road connections could be made with the large village of Colmonell and the holiday resort of Ballantrae where the river reaches the sea. The crossing loop was retained until 1992.

The railway now begins to rise again steeply, mostly at between 1 in 67 and 1 in 73, following the course of the Duisk and, after a while, gradually moving away from it to the right up the hillside. Splendid views to the north-east and east now begin to open up, with the great hills of Shalloch-on-Minnoch and the Merrick (the latter being the highest hill in southern Scotland) standing out magnificently. Two large viaducts, one over the Lig Burn and the other near Daltangan farm, across a steep dip in the hillside near the 12th milepost are crossed, and several rock cuttings are threaded before Barrhill station is reached, the village of Barrhill, on the main road to Newton Stewart, lying well down in the Duisk valley two-thirds of a mile to the left. This is the only station now open between Girvan and Stranraer, and all trains now halt here. It is now the most convenient changing point for Newton Stewart and the country to the south of it; what were once sidings are now places for car-parking, and buses run from the village three-quarters of a mile distant. The station buildings are small and the platforms somewhat short. The large water tank that formerly stood here for the replenishment of steam locomotives' tenders has now been dismantled. The longest trains now to use the station have only four coaches, whereas during the 1930s trains of from nine to ten coaches might draw up here, and crossing one of these with a freight train could cause quite a problem.

The signal box at present in use at Barrhill is unusual in having done duty elsewhere. In 1935 its predecessor was destroyed by fire; shortly before that happened the box at Portpatrick had become redundant following a decision to work that branch on the 'one engine in steam' principle. So it was dismantled and re-erected at Barrhill.

The line now turns to the south-west to traverse the wild moorland separating the basin of the Duisk from that of the Water of Luce. It first follows the Cross Water, one of the Duisk's tributaries, for a couple of miles through barren country which was formerly more open and bare but has now been much afforested. One is now approaching the summit of the line,

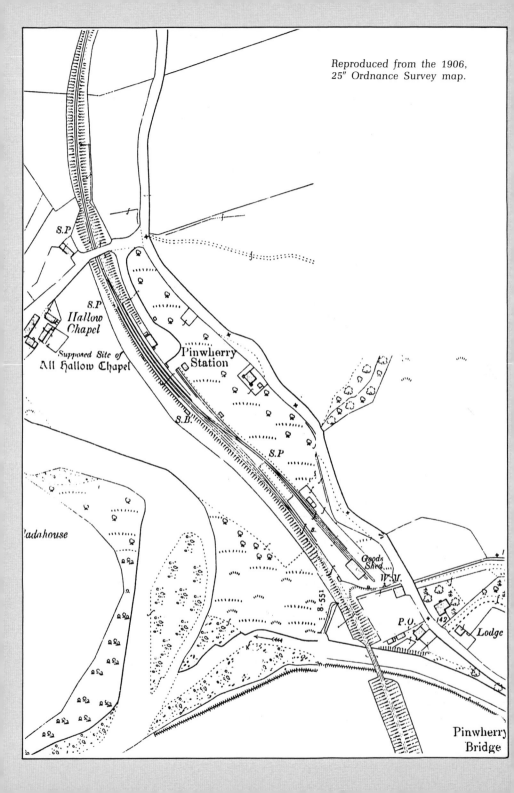

Reproduced from the 1906,
25″ Ordnance Survey map.

A beautiful photograph of 4−4−0 tender locomotive No. 14510 entering Girvan station in September 1934.   *E.R. Morten*

A general view of Girvan station in July 1957 (note the water tower, now removed). A Stanier 'Black Five' waits at the head of the morning train from Glasgow.
H.C. Casserley

Girvan No. 2 signal box situated at the end of the platform. *Photomatic Ltd*

A special consignment of nitro-chalk fertiliser sent from Heysham to Stranraer on 26th August, 1965. Two 'Black Fives', Nos. 44724 and 44727, were selected to haul it from Ayr onwards, but when it came to Glendoune bank, beyond Girvan, they could not get it more than part of the way up to Pinmore, and had to leave half the train behind, coming back for it after they had taken the front half to Pinwherry and left it in a siding. From Pinwherry onwards the grades are rather less difficult and it was possible to take the whole train through. The photograph shows the reunited train leaving Pinwherry, where it has just crossed with a northbound passenger train. Bob Smillie, who contributed memories of his days as a fireman on this line (*see Chapter 10*) was driving the pilot engine, No. 44724. *D. Cross*

Pinmore station, seen here in July 1968, after the removal of the passing loop and the up platform.   *J.P. Alsop*

Earlier in July 1957, Pinmore station was still active with passengers walking its platform over-looked by the very high situation of the signal box.   *H.C. Casserley*

Two views, taken in April 1948, of Pinwherry station looking in opposite directions. The top view shows the 'unusual' addition of the bathroom to the station building, whilst the lower photograph shows the down platform, station yard and buildings plus the wooden part of the up platform. (The line is actually *level* at this point – *see page 29.*)

H.C. Casserley and H.B. Priestley

A study in reflections! Barrhill station from the train in July 1957, showing the substantial water tank and tower, with the goods yard beyond. *H.C. Casserley*

The sparse up platform at Barrhill station on 15th July, 1968. *J.P. Alsop*

The rear of the station buildings at Glenwhilly showing the bleak nature of the area, photographed in July 1957.
H.C. Casserley

Glenwhilly station photographed on the same day showing the ornate large platform lamps and the single line tablet apparatus at the end of each platform.
H.C. Casserley

Glenwhilly signal box in July 1957.
H.C. Casserley

New Luce station down platform and station buildings in the 1960s.   *H.B. Priestley*

The up platform at New Luce taken from a down train on 23rd June, 1962. Note the wooden platform.   *H.C. Casserley*

Stranraer station before rebuilding, showing the car ferry boat *Dalriada* with its bows raised to take vehicles on board before its journey to Ireland, on 12th October, 1977. Note the station is very busy.   *Ross Cunningham*

Day train from Carlisle arriving at Stranraer in September 1978 behind an unidentified class '47' diesel locomotive.   *Ross Cunningham*

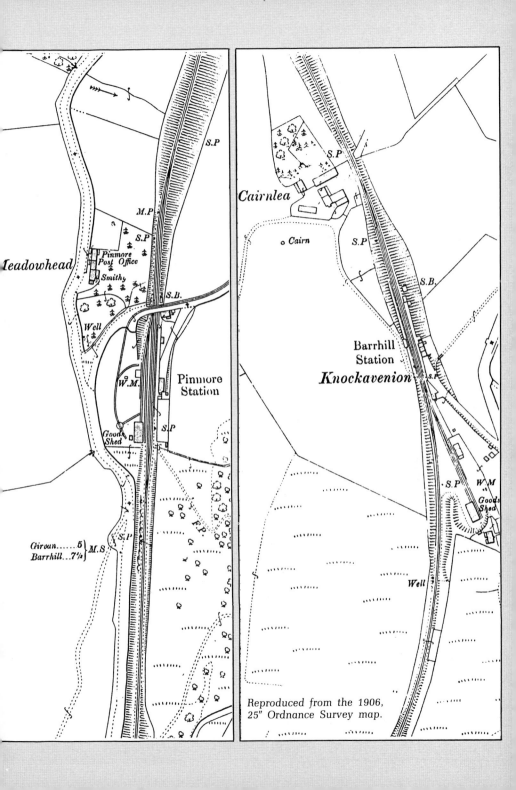

Reproduced from the 1906, 25″ Ordnance Survey map.

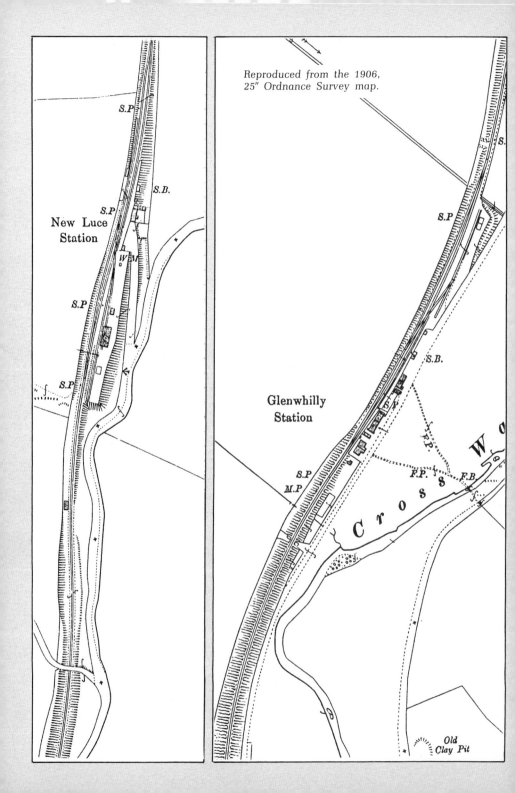

Reproduced from the 1906,
25" Ordnance Survey map.

New Luce
Station

Glenwhilly
Station

Old
Clay Pit

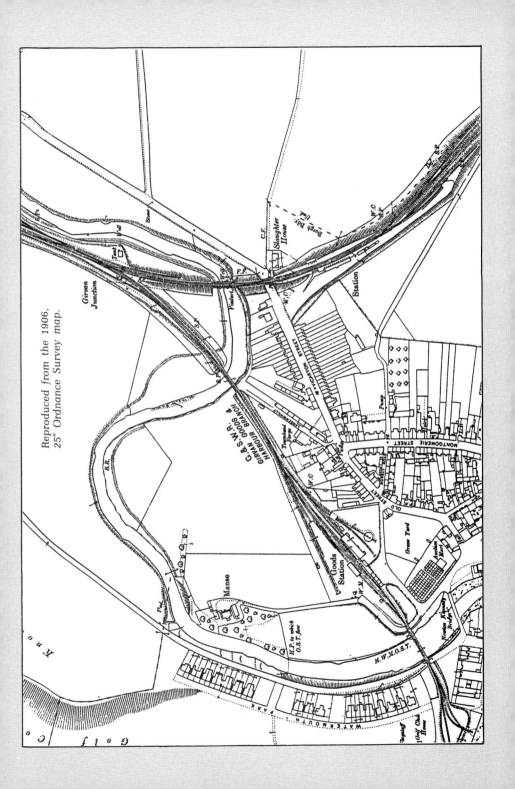

Reproduced from the 1906,
25″ Ordnance Survey map.

and all around is bleak and uninhabited. The remains of former railway-men's cottages are passed at a point where a rough track leads eastwards to the narrow metalled road linking Barrhill with New Luce, and at milepost 16½ Chirmorie summit, 690 ft above sea level, is reached. One is now nearly half-way to Stranraer.

The descent, across moorland still as wild as it has ever been, since afforestation has not yet reached that far, continues for 4½ miles at 1 in 100 or thereabouts. The line is making for the valley of the Cross Water of Luce, and eventually curves south into it, and crosses the stream four times by three large bridges and a smaller one. These provided an indication for engine crews of the nearness of Glenwhilly station; when the night was pitch-black and nothing could be seen, they listened for 'three long rumbles and a short one.'

At Glenwhilly there was formerly a station with a passing loop; the latter with its signal box is still there but the station is gone. Not many passengers could have used it when it was there as it is near no village and the countryside around is bare of habitations. The loop is still needed because of the distance from the one at Barrhill and the steepness of the intervening gradients; as things are the block section, at just over 8 miles, is long enough, and in the days of steam a goods train could take over half an hour to traverse it.

The Cross Water of Luce now turns sharply to the south-east, and the line leaves it and cuts its way through an intervening ridge, making a sudden sharp rise at 1 in 77 for ⅓ mile before continuing to fall at an even steeper gradient. This includes 3 miles at 1 in 57 and 1 in 58, and at its lower end forms the dreaded 'Swan's Neck', an S-curve that needs great care in descending and which was a terror to northbound trains in bad weather. Here, more than anywhere else on the line, trains in the days of steam have been brought to a dead stand, their crews then being obliged to divide the load in order to get both parts separately to Glenwhilly. As one leaves the 'Swan's Neck' one is in the valley of the Main Water of Luce, which is now followed almost to its mouth on the shore of Luce Bay.

After crossing this stream by a ten-arched viaduct the site of New Luce station is reached. This was closed in 1965 and demolished in 1971. It was the last one on the original line going south and had two staggered platforms and a passing loop long enough to take a freight train of 29 wagons. The village itself lies in the valley about half a mile to the north-east, where the Main and Cross Waters of Luce make their junction. The line, now on generally easier gradients, continues along the right bank of the Water of Luce, falling for 5½ miles with one slight intermediate hump until the site of Challoch Junction is reached. A mile and a half short of the latter, as one emerges from a cutting, one can see on the left across a stream the ruined remains of Glenluce Abbey, a Cistercian monastery founded at the end of the 12th century.

The line now turns to the east, and it needs a careful inspection of the ground through the left-hand windows of the train to see where the Portpatrick Railway came in to join it, the signal box, points and crossing loop having all now gone. A mile and a half further on is the site of Dunragit

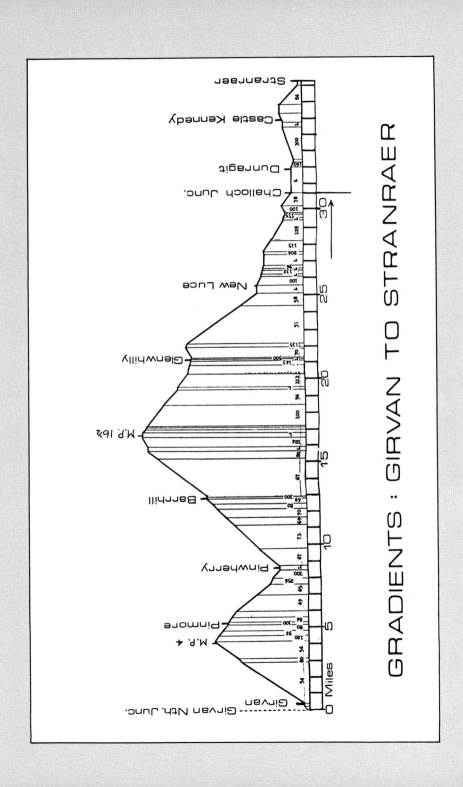

GRADIENTS : GIRVAN TO STRANRAER

station and signal box; the latter is still needed because the A748 road crosses the line on the level at this point and there are gates to be operated. Castle Kennedy station was a further three miles towards Stranraer, and has now also gone. Both stations were substantial structures, and Castle Kennedy even boasted a 'Ladies' Waiting Room', as was only proper when one considered the nearness of the Castle itself, the seat of the Earl of Stair. Between them the line was double-tracked for a while, the widening having been done, as related in the last chapter, during World War II; it has now been singled again. After the gentle rise to Castle Kennedy a steep fall follows for a mile to Stranraer Town station, where most trains formerly terminated and where the connection could be made to Portpatrick. Stranraer Town has now been closed, together with the Portpatrick branch, but its sidings still fan out beyond the point where the branch to the Harbour diverged to the right.

Stranraer Harbour is now the town's only station, where all the trains from Girvan terminate. It is quite an impressive structure, with a canopied roof over the one of its two platforms which is usually used, and has a covered way leading to the point where the boats for Larne can be boarded. From the platforms' further ends there is a splendid prospect towards the mouth of Loch Ryan, through which the ferry boats, of which there are several sailings each day, pass before turning west for Ulster.

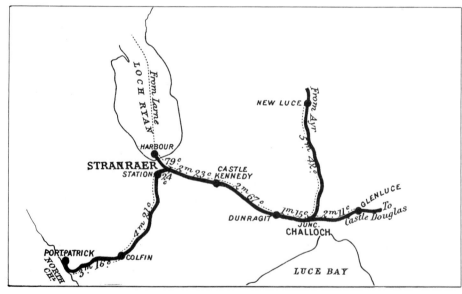

The Girvan and the Portpatrick line join at Challoch Junction , reproduced from the 1907, Railway Clearing House Junction diagram map.

Chapter Six

Train Services and Passenger Accommodation: 1877–1965

An examination of successive timetables for the Girvan–Stranraer line shows, as might have been expected, a gradual improvement in frequency and amenities up to the outbreak of World War I, a subsequent lessening, a recovery during the inter-war years, another falling-off during World War II, and a certain amount of improvement later in the face of bus competition and the increasing use of the private car. In 1965 evolution was replaced by revolution, and eventually a very different kind of railway emerged, so the present chapter takes that year as its point of termination.

From 1877 to 1881 the passenger services on the G&PJR were a well spaced-out sequence of four trains each way daily, the first southbound one and the last northbound one connecting with the steamer to and from Larne and not stopping intermediately except at Pinwherry and Dunragit. Two, including the boat train, ran through to or from Glasgow; the other two connected with Glasgow trains at Girvan Old station and joined or left the new line at Girvan North Junction. The boat trains took between 71 and 75 minutes for the complete journey, the others between 15 and 20 minutes longer, depending on their periods of waiting at intermediate stations in order to cross other trains. Timings between stations reflected the difficulty of the road; the 4.9 miles between Girvan New station and Pinmore, for example, since it was so steeply uphill amost the whole way, were allowed 13 minutes, but only 10 minutes in the opposite direction. Exact timekeeping within sections was no doubt never aimed at, for some of the intermediate stages were generously scheduled, and on them time lost could be recovered.

The period between February 1882 and August 1883, when the line from Challoch Junction to Stranraer was closed to G&PJR trains, saw the latter's services reduced to two each way daily, New Luce being the southern terminus at which connections to or from Stranraer were made by horse-drawn carriages. A single set of coaches sufficed for the service, which took between 55 minutes and an hour either way to or from Girvan, stopping at all four intermediate stations. Engine and coaches were stabled overnight at New Luce, and after the first return trip almost six hours elapsed before the second one. One engine crew and one guard sufficed for the service, which took up well over 12 hours between preparing the engine in the morning and stabling it at night. During the long break in the middle of the day the ancient locomotive was presumably given some servicing. It is interesting to note that the time needed for the road journey between New Luce and Stranraer was well over an hour for the 12 miles, whereas the trains did twice that distance in less time. Things were to be very different when the age of the petrol engine arrived.

The resumption of the through services to Stranraer brought a reversion to the former pattern of four trains daily each way. In 1886 a note appeared in the timetable to the effect that the G&SWR did not book passengers beyond Girvan. This reflected the new situation. The G&PJR was now operating its own trains with its own locomotives and coaches, and none ran through to Glasgow. For a short while the service became distinctly slower, particularly in 1886 when the only locomotives available were antiquated ex-North London Railway tanks. Two 0–6–0 tender locomotives which were supplied later enabled a slight improvement. This state of affairs continued until the end of 1891.

The following year the line was bought by the G&SWR and improvement was soon seen. In that year an extra limited-stop service was put on during the summer to and from Glasgow, taking three hours each way from and to Stranraer, and a fast evening service, connecting with the late afternoon boat from Larne, appeared in the up direction. This eventually was to develop into the famous 'Paddy' which got passengers from Belfast into Glasgow round about midnight. From 1897 extra Saturday services began to appear, while the proto-Paddy turned into the real thing, a light and fast train which reached Girvan non-stop in an hour from Stranraer Harbour. After the turn of the century the Girvan stop was made conditional instead of being obligatory, and the departure time from Stranraer became 9.55 pm. The train was now accelerated to an 83-minute run to Ayr, at an average speed of almost 43 mph, which does not look much on paper, but when the gradients are borne in mind, and the need to slow several times to exchange tablets, it appears almost a counsel of perfection, and indeed could only have been performed with the light load that was customary.

For a while the 'Paddy' became the most exciting train on which one could travel within Scotland, for drivers made it a point of honour to recover as much time as possible if a late arrival of the boat from Larne delayed their start. Risks were certainly taken at some of the passing loops, the permitted speed being considerably exceeded. This went on until, as narrated above, the fatal accident to another boat train near Salisbury caused Manson to issue a stern warning against such a practice, and the crews had to repress their enthusiasm. Nevertheless the timing remained unchanged for another five years, after which eight minutes were added to it.

By 1914 the pattern of services had improved to six each way on summer Saturdays, but World War I compelled a diminution first to four, then during 1917–1918 to three daily. The 'Paddy', though not shown in the timetable, continued to run, since there was so much extra passenger traffic because of the stationing of military personnel in Northern Ireland. Things improved in 1919, when this train was once again publicly advertised, though on a distinctly slower timing than before, Glasgow not being reached till after 1 am. A note in the timetable also showed that passengers who took the 4.10 pm service from Glasgow to Stranraer could be accommodated on the boat in sleeping berths, the actual crossing being made on the early morning sailing. This reflected the fact that the newest steamer on the crossing offered such accommodation. It was a considerable convenience for Belfast-bound passengers who did not wish to waste a whole day over the journey or alternatively be put to the trouble of finding hotel accommodation in Stranraer. This facility remained until quite recently.

By 1922 the number of southbound trains had increased to five, though there were only four northbound, the 'Paddy' having for some reason been temporarily discontinued. It returned, however, the following year, much decelerated from its pre-war timings, for it was now a much heavier train.

The line had now passed under LMS ownership, and the next 16 years were to see many improvements, including the provision of restaurant cars in some trains and the general use of vestibuled corridor coaches. Speeds did not increase since it was not yet possible to match increasing loads with locomotives of commensurate power, because of the small size of the Stranraer turntable. Additional week-end services were also put on during the summer months, and a later train from Glasgow, reaching Stranraer just before 11 pm, gave the would-be occupier of a berth on the boat a much more convenient connecting service. In 1932 the practice began of naming some of the trains; the 12.30 pm up from Stranraer became 'The Fast Belfast' and the following year the 'Paddy', slightly speeded up, became officially 'The Irishman'.

Until 1927 there had been no Sunday trains at all on the Girvan–Stranraer line, in accordance with the long-standing usage of Sabbath observance in Scotland – something which is now confined to the remoter parts of the West and North and to the Hebrides, where the disapproving writs of kirk ministers still run. Nonetheless, largely in consequence of World War I, when conflict could not be restricted to weekdays, restraints were beginning to loosen, and in any case buses were plying on Sundays to let the public have a chance of an outing on their free day. In June 1927 the railway began to run Sunday excursions, beginning with a trip from Glasgow to Portpatrick and back. Patronage was unexpectedly large, and on the first occasion so many coaches were needed that, despite being double-headed, the train could not keep to its set times; after that larger locomotives were provided. Eventually the Sunday summer excursion train became an institution, running one week to Portpatrick and the next to Stranraer Harbour, at which place the excursionists boarded one of the steamers and were taken for a cruise to Bangor, on Belfast Lough, and back. This latter trip became very popular; on one occasion in 1934, 16 coaches were required – which must have been the longest train ever to have run over this line in peace-time.

By 1939 the Girvan–Stranraer service reached its peak, heavy trains being regularly double-headed. The outbreak of World War II ended this spell of prosperity, and emphasis had again to be placed on military necessity rather than commercial profitability. The mid-day boat services were discontinued, as also was the late evening service from Glasgow; the 'Paddy' was decelerated but continued to run. The other trains, which called at all stations, continued on schedules much the same as in 1939. Patronage of the boat trains was largely that of service personnel going on or off leave from their duties in Ulster. As the war continued, punctuality deteriorated and inadequate maintenance of the passenger stock made every journey something of an ordeal. With the return of peace the cancelled services were restored, but pre-war standards of service could not be brought back so readily. In the words of David L. Smith,

> The railways were left to make the best of a very bad job, with equipment in a sorry state, profitable wartime tasks at an end, and a reputation to rebuild with a public which, having suffered all sorts of privations of travel during war, were only too ready to desert to road transport.*

---

*D.L. Smith: *The Little Railways of South-West Scotland*: pp. 191–192.

The timetable for the Girvan–Stranraer route in 1948, the first year of operation by British Railways, shows a return to the pattern of four trains each way daily, one being the up 'Paddy' on a surprisingly fast 60-minute timing inclusive of a stop at Barrhill. Ten years later things had further improved, with an extra up mid-day service returning from Glasgow to reach Stranraer at 10.05 pm, both having boat connections; timings all round were also slightly faster.

In 1959 the shape of things to come began to manifest itself. BR had already taken the decision to phase out the steam locomotive, and in that year the whole passenger service between Girvan and Stranraer became diesel-operated, with multiple-unit trains. They were satisfactory enough when they did not break down, but they lacked the resilience of steam traction; if one of the motors gave out they could not manage the gradients and an improvised steam service had to be substituted. Meanwhile Sunday trains had reappeared, evening boat services being put on in each direction. However, the special Sunday excursions did not come back.

So much for passenger services. Freight traffic was, on this line, of lesser importance, particularly when goods were increasingly being sent to Stranraer on motor lorries. Quite early in the line's existence, after the G & SWR take-over in 1892, one through freight train had begun to operate, first at midnight, later at 1 am, from College Yard, Glasgow, to Stranraer, returning between 6 and 7 pm. With freight trains the passage of the Girvan–Stranraer section was necessarily slow, partly because the trains were not continuously braked and partly because it was often necessary to stop to attach or detach a van or wagon. Something like twice as much time as passenger trains took was needed to cover the distance. This pair of trains, supplemented occasionally by others, especially during the war years, sufficed to serve the area and deal with such goods as were shipped from or into Stranraer.

The quality of passenger accommodation improved over the years from the earliest ex-North London Railway four-wheeled boxes. In 1889 the Ayrshire and Wigtownshire Railway (as the line, for a brief period, was now called) took delivery of six 6-wheelers, liveried in varnished teak, newly-built by Craven Brothers of Sheffield, and these were used on through trains to and from Glasgow; this was possible since they were fitted with continuous brakes. In 1892, after the G & SWR had taken over the line, the decision was made to scrap the old North London carriages, but to retain the newly-built ones, which were sent to other parts of the G & SWR system, other 6-wheelers taking their places.

In 1899 a set of three bogie corridor carriages was specially built at Kilmarnock by the G & SWR for use between Glasgow and Stranraer; they were employed on the mid-day up boat train and returned on the evening express due at Stranraer at 8 pm. A few years later a similar set was put into service on the up 'Paddy' which left Stranraer Harbour at 9.55 pm and made the break-neck journeys referred to above. Non-bogie coaches now began to be phased out from the main line services, though the six-wheelers were still used when times were busy.

With the absorption of the G & SWR into the LMS it became possible for carriage stock from other parts of the latter system to be cascaded elsewhere and vehicles built at Derby and Crewe began to appear. In all trains corridor stock soon predominated, and for the first time restaurant cars were included. Ex-L&NWR dining saloons and ex-CR Pullman cars that had been used as diners began to appear. The former were massive and luxuriously appointed, with first and third class sections and a kitchen between them. Each was 65½ ft long, ran on 6-wheeled bogies and had a clerestory roof. Built from 1896 onwards, they had been used in West Coast expresses between Euston and Scotland. Now re-liveried in LMS crimson lake, they no longer looked as gorgeous as before, but rode smoothly and were popular with their patrons. The former Pullmans were from a batch of nine that the CR had used as diners without requiring an extra supplement. Built in 1914, they were eventually sold by the Pullman Car Company to the LMS, who reliveried them in crimson lake. They too were steady-riding 12-wheelers.

The only notable change in the coaching stock thenceforward on the Stranraer line was the introduction of steel-panelled LMS passenger stock of successive designs, most having end doors and large single windows in the compartments. From 1959, however, diesel multiple units replaced the steam-hauled coaches, when the 3-car sets built for BR at Swindon were put on the line. Only one car in each set was compartmented, the other two being saloons. A 3-car unit now generally sufficed for each train, passenger demand having fallen off greatly from what it had been before the war. For a time a small buffet section was installed in each unit, but there proved to be no great demand for this facility and it was soon removed.

Advertisement from Bradshaw's Guide for April 1910

Chapter Seven
Locomotives Used Between 1877 and 1922

At first glance it might appear that a disproportionate part of this book is devoted to considering the locomotives used on this line. The excuse must be the very great variety of motive power seen in the past over these 38 miles of track. Railway enthusiasts in general find locomotives more interesting than any other aspect of railway operation. If one is going to write about them at all, therefore, one is bound to do it at some length, since so many different types were successively employed.

The first engines to work the line during the first period of G&SWR operation belonged to the latter company, and the numbers of some are known as well as their allocations to particular trains. These are set out below in tabular form; fuller details of the locomotives can be found in Appendix III.

No.	Type	Designer	Date built	How used
71	2−4−0	J. Stirling	9/1870	On 7.15 am Stranraer−Glasgow as far as Ayr, returning with 4.15 pm from Glasgow to Stranraer.
240	0−4−2	"	4/1875	Freight trains, Glasgow−Stranraer and back.
83	2−4−0	"	6/1889	On 7 am Glasgow−Stranraer, returning with 8.15 pm Stranraer−Glasgow.
158	2−4−0	Smellie	12/1879	Replacing No. 71 on duty as above.
76	2−4−0	J. Stirling	7/1870	Passenger trains, Stranraer & back.
17	0−6−0	J. Stirling	5/1878	Night freight train, Glasgow−Stranraer, returning next day.
159	0−6−0	"	5/1878	Alternating with No. 17 on same duty.

From February 1882, when the Portpatrick Railway closed its line to the G&PJR beyond Challoch Junction, the two daily trains in each direction between Girvan and New Luce were operated by a single 2−4−0, which had to travel tender-first for half its time − not an enviable proposition during the winter. A single freight train was also worked from Girvan to New Luce and back daily during this period, the locomotive being either No. 145 or 148, each being a domeless 0−4−2 designed by Patrick Stirling and built in 1866. Neither of these engines had a continuous braking system, so they could only be used on freight trains, and needed to proceed very cautiously south of Ayr to avoid coupling-breakage on one of the steep inclines if slack links were suddenly tightened.

In August 1883 the full service to Stranraer was resumed for a further 2½ years. Then came the G&PJR's decision to work the line on its own. The latter's first needs were to obtain locomotives and rolling stock from a suitable source, which they eventually found far afield when, in June 1886, the North London Railway sold them three 4−4−0 outside-cylindered tank engines built in 1861. A number of passenger coaches and goods vehicles, all four-wheeled, were obtained from the same source, as mentioned in the previous chapter. The locomotives were numbered 1, 2 and 3. In addition a small saddle-tank engine was obtained from the English contractor, I.W. Boulton. It was a diminutive machine with driving wheels only 3 feet in diameter, and it does not seem to have lasted very long. Probably it was required for hauling vehicles to or from the quay at Stranraer. With this scanty assortment the G&PJR maintained a precarious service for five months, until it also received two new 0−6−0s from Neilson & Co., of Glasgow, which were numbered 4 and 5. They had domed boilers, but the cabs were of Stirling's 'wrap-over' pattern; an unusual feature was the hand-rail along each tender side, associated with foot-boards below at about axle-level; one wonders why these should have been thought necessary.

The next phase of the line's existence, following its sale and re-naming as the Ayrshire and Wigtownshire Railway, saw two more 0−6−0s added to the stock, built by the Clyde Locomotive Company of Glasgow and substantially the same as the two from Neilson, but having a somewhat different style of cab with more overhead protection; these were numbered 6 and 7.

For some five years these seven engines operated the trains between Girvan and Stranraer, the ex-NLR tanks wearing themselves out in the process until only No. 1 remained, Nos. 2 and 3 having been cannibalised to provide it with replacement parts. Before being sent north their 850-gallon tanks had sufficed for the short end-to-end journeys on the North London line, but in between Girvan and Stranraer they needed to take water at least twice, at Pinwherry, Barrhill, Glenwhilly or Challoch.

With the resumption of G&SWR operation in 1892 the condition of all the locomotives was revealed in a report by James Manson, whose findings have already been alluded to in Chapter 3. Only one of the three 4−4−0 tanks was now in working order, and only two of the 0−6−0s. Carrying on as before was out of the question; there had to be replacements. The four usable 0−6−0s (two needing first to be reconditioned) continued for a while to work on passenger trains between Girvan and Stranraer, while goods engines of the G&SWR, built by Smellie, took over the freight services, one being shedded at Ayr, one at Stranraer and one at Glasgow.

These latter engines were also 0−6−0s, built in 1888−1889, with 5 ft 1½ in. driving wheels. In their original form they were domeless, Smellie having continued Stirling's practice in this respect, but Manson later rebuilt them with rather larger domed boilers, larger firegrates and a slightly increased working pressure. They steamed and ran well, but the specially-devised steam-operated brakes fitted by Smellie were not at first satisfactory and required re-modelling. They continued to be used on freight trains between Glasgow and Stranraer until the eve of World War I.

Round about this time the G&SWR, formerly a user of the Westinghouse brake, decided to change to the vacuum brake, which the Midland Railway used, once it began to take over through trains from that company at Carlisle. All the Ayrshire and Wigtownshire engines were Westinghouse-braked, so rather than go to the expense of adapting them it was decided to confine them to freight work.

All the passenger trains were now entrusted to G&SWR engines. Initially some of Smellie's 'Wee Bogies' were drafted for that purpose. Built between 1882 and 1885, they were domeless 4−4−0s with driving wheels 6 ft 1 in. in diameter, and had originally been used on the steeply-graded Glasgow −Greenock line. On the still steeper banks of the Glasgow−Stranraer route they were required to work hard on quicker schedules, though with lighter loads. They remained on these duties until 1897. In appearance they resembled James Stirling's engines, having 'wrap-over' cab roofs and smokebox wing-plates. They also had larger cylinders than any engine previously built for this railway.

After a few years they were replaced by some of the more powerful 4−4−0s of Manson's '8' class, which had been designed as express engines for use on the main Glasgow−Kilmarnock−Carlisle route. Built between 1892 and 1897, they were not on the face of it suitable machines for use on gradients as steep as those on the Stranraer road, their coupled wheels being as large as 6 ft 9½ in. in diameter. They were Manson's first design for the G&SWR and much resembled those he had previously built for the GNSR, except for the larger driving wheels. Unlike Stirling's and Smellie's engines they had domed boilers, bogies with 'swing-link' attachments and cab roofs extending further back than those of the earlier engines. In spite of the size of their coupled wheels, with light loads the line south of Girvan held no terrors for them. In the first decade of the present century, when the evening 'Paddy' was required to run non-stop from Stranraer to Ayr, instances occurred when an '8' class engine recovered time by covering the 59 miles in 76 to 78 minutes, inclusive of slacks to exchange tablets. Their limit for timekeeping runs on this train was 150 tons.

These large-wheeled locomotives continued to dominate the Girvan− Stranraer services until Manson's retirement in 1912, but a smaller-wheeled variation also occasionally put in an appearance. This type was built be- tween 1895 and 1899; in it the driving wheel diameter was reduced to 6 ft 1 in. and the boiler pressure was slightly increased. These, like Smellie's 'Wee Bogies', were originally built for use on the Greenock line and were generally known as 'Greenock Bogies'. Some of them later found their ways to other parts of the G&SWR system and a few were shedded at Girvan and Stranraer.

Manson's successor, Peter Drummond, formerly locomotive superinten- dent on the Highland Railway and younger brother of the celebrated Dugald Drummond of the L&SWR, tended in his own designs to perpetuate features that his brother had employed. In 1915 three of his super-heated '137' class 4−4−0s, shedded at Ayr, began to work through to Stranraer. They were certainly successful at hauling the trains, coping easily with the tough inclines and consuming very little coal, but here as elsewhere they proved too heavy for the track and were removed to work on the main line from Glasgow to Carlisle. In their places Drummond's earlier unsuperheated '131' class were tried, but they showed themselves inferior to the Manson engines in every way, and were especially heavy on coal. So the latter were brought back to operate such train services as wartime exigencies dictated. Later, in LMS days, these two Drummond types came back again to the Stranraer road, as related in the next chapter.

Chapter Eight
Locomotives Used Between 1922 and 1966

With the submergence of the G & SWR into the LMS system the one-time Girvan and Portpatrick Junction Railway became a small part of a very much larger company, and policy regarding the use of locomotives and rolling stock was henceforward determined in England. Such a change might have seemed a matter for regret, but things had not gone well in the locomotive department of the G & SWR since Manson had retired in 1912. To the disruption caused by the war were added what many felt to be the mistakes of Manson's two successors. One had built a number of unsuitable engines as well as a few good ones; the other had rebuilt existing ones and spoiled them in so doing. D.L. Smith, the historian of G & SWR locomotive development and use, expressed his feelings thus:

> Those final years of the G & SW had not been happy ones. Sick at heart with the Whitelegg regime, I turned with a high hope to this great new idea, this 'Grouping', which promised us light in our darkness.*

Smith was hoping that the engines from other parts of the LMS system might be made available for work in Scotland, and especially on the G & SWR line, for passenger, goods and mixed traffic work. The resources of the former L & NWR and MR could now be tapped, and engines of Crewe or Derby design might be expected to be sent north to work Scottish services, particularly if new construction at those places displaced existing engines for work elsewhere.

What actually happened was not quite what was expected. In the struggle for power and influence that occurred between the main locomotive departments of the LMS's two chief constituent companies, Derby ousted Crewe as the originator of locomotive types, and an existing design, with only slight alterations, was selected for multiplication in large numbers. This was the celebrated 3-cylindered 'Midland Compound' 4-4-0. It was newly-built members of this class that first came north to head express trains on the former CR and G & SWR, and they won golden opinions from those who drove them once the technique of working them had been mastered. But this took time, and on former G & SWR metals existing locomotives had to continue for some while.

For handling the freight services between Glasgow and Stranraer recourse was had to former G & SWR 0-6-0s, some of P. Drummond's '279' class being sent to Ayr, from which place they took over the 1 am goods train from Glasgow to Stranraer, returning on an evening freight service. As first built these locomotives had some unusual features. Drummond, copying his brother's practice on the L & SWR, had installed a feed water heating system in the tender, to which exhaust steam taken from the base of the blast pipe in the smokebox was conducted by pipes to give up its remaining heat to the water in the tank; the latter was then fed into the boiler by pressure from steam pumps situated between the second and third pair of coupled wheels. For this reason these engines were always colloquially known as 'Pumpers', even after the equipment had been removed during 1918–1922. At the time of their construction they were the heaviest 0-6-0s in Britain, and in their original state they were not at all satisfactory, being heavy on coal, consuming huge amounts of oil and having connecting rods which were always

---

*David L. Smith: *Legends of the Glasgow & South Western Railway in LMS days*: p. 5. In preparing this chapter I have been much indebted to this racy and readable book, and recommend it unreservedly.

running hot. By 1925, when the first of them was sent to Ayr, modifications had been made to their big-end bearings which lessened the tendency to overheat. They tackled the freight trains reasonably well, and could run fast downhill, but were sluggish climbers.

In addition to these, one of Drummond's later 2–6–0s also found its way to the Girvan–Stranraer line during 1924, to take its turn on the 1 am freight service from Glasgow. This was No. 61, now re-numbered by the LMS as No. 17823. Engines of this class, while slightly heavier than the 'Pumpers', each had a leading pony truck, so that the coupled wheels took less of the burden and the whole engine was kinder to the track. It performed more satisfactorily than the 0–6–0s, for Drummond had learned by his mistakes, left out some of the controversial features of the earlier engines and given the new class superheating. His successor R.H. Whitelegg had also made some slight modifications. However, it too was prone to run hot in its bearings.

Drummond, as mentioned in the previous chapter, had also built two types of passenger 4–4–0s, in 1913 and 1915 – the former without, the latter with, superheating equipment. Both were very heavy and liable to do damage to the permanent way, so were prohibited from using the route from Dumfries to Stranraer. However, after the LMS had strengthened the latter it was possible to use them between Girvan and Stranraer, and as reconstructed they did reasonably good work, but were still prone to overheat in their bearings. They retained this fault right up to the time of their withdrawal, and one other in addition, a tendency for the bogie to seize unexpectedly on the surface of the under-frame, which it supported, because of inadequate lubrication. This at times could almost cause a derailment. Smith refers to such an event when, between Chirmorie summit and Barrhill,

> . . . as the engine entered the Gunner's Cut No. 14521 gave a furious lurch, and from beneath the bogie came 'a thing like three smiddy fires.' The driver thought she had gone off the rails and back on.*

In the summer of 1928 two Midland compounds were put on the Stranraer road, Nos. 1181 and 1182; they were later followed by 1179 and 1180. These were from the large number that had been built following a decision at Derby to build nearly 200 of them for service over the whole LMS system as standard express engines for light trains. Once the special way of working them had been learned they performed feats of haulage in Scotland greater than had ever been expected of them on the former MR system.

Train loadings on the expresses from and to Glasgow which connected with the steamers at Larne were increasing, with corridor stock and a dining car being often included. On this road the permitted limit for a Midland compound was 200 tons; above that figure a pilot engine was supposed to be provided. However, loads well above that level were sometimes taken by a single locomotive, and time was kept – admittedly on rather easier schedules than in G&SWR days. The compounds did have one fault, a tendency to slip. This was accentuated on the Girvan–Stranraer road not only by the steepness of the gradients (the southbound start from Girvan being especially difficult) but also by the superelevation of the outer rails on the curves, which in places was as great as 5½ inches. This made for safer and more

---

*D.L. Smith: *Legends of the G&SWR in LMS days*: p. 19.

One of the two 0–6–0 tender locomotives (No. 5) bought by the G&PJR from the Clyde Locomotive Company in 1887, to operate both passenger and goods trains during the short period when it ran its own services before being absorbed into the G&SWR. Note the handrails on the tender sides and the footboards below the tender springs.

Author's Collection

No. 185 was one of Hugh Smellie's '157' class of 2–4–0, tender locomotives as used on passenger trains between Glasgow and Stranraer during 1880–1882. Smellie continued the Stirling tradition of domeless boilers and 'wrap-over' open cabs.

Author's Collection

Seen here in LMS days as No. 14126, this 4–4–0 tender locomotive was one of Hugh Smellie's 'Wee Bogies' as rebuilt by Manson and used on Glasgow–Stranraer trains between 1892 and 1897.

Author's Collection

A Manson '8' class 4–4–0 tender locomotive, No. 8, with 6 ft 9½ inch coupled wheels, as used at the turn of the century between Glasgow and Stranraer, where with light trains they performed well, even over the heavy gradients south of Girvan and in spite of the size of their coupled wheels.   *Author's Collection*

A Drummond 'Pumper' 0–6–0 tender locomotive, No. 300, as originally built in 1913, with a feed-water-heating system in the tender, from which the heated water was forced into the boiler by pumps – hence the engine's nickname, which persisted even after the pumps had been removed. In their original form they were abject failures; rebuilding improved them, but they were sluggish engines and readily over-heated their bearings.   *Author's Collection*

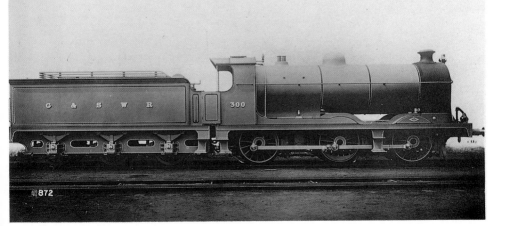

Drummond 4–4–0 LMS No. 14514 (originally No. 135 on the G&SWR) built without superheating equipment but superheated in 1926, after which it was used on the Girvan to Stranraer line and did reasonably good work, though still prone to overheat its main bearings.   *Author's Collection*

Drummond 4–4–0 No. 14520, superheated from the beginning, and originally No. 151 on the G&SWR. This type proved to be too heavy for the G&SWR track, but after the latter was strengthened in LMS days it was used successfully for a while on the Girvan to Stranraer line before being ousted by the 4–4–0 Midland Compounds.   *Author's Collection*

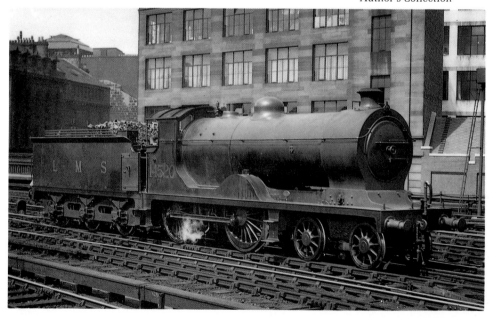

One of Fowler's class '2P' 4–4–0 tender locomotives, built at Derby in 1928, which is seen here at St Enoch station, Glasgow, at the head of a train for Stranraer. These engines were very much liked by their crews and referred to as 'the wee black yins'. Though not by any means greyhounds, they were reliable and light on maintenance and repairs. Note the brakes on the bogie wheels. *Author's Collection*

No. 2870 was one of Hughes' 2–6–0 mixed traffic, tender engines, originally designed before Fowler succeeded him as Chief Mechanical Engineer on the LMS; the latter made only a few slight changes. Despite their ungainly appearance, which gained for them the nickname of 'Crabs', these engines, introduced on to the Glasgow–Stranraer services, were much liked because of their ability to tackle the heavy gradients and even reach 70 mph on passenger trains. They were the largest engines that could be used on this line, before the fitting of an enlarged turntable at Stranraer. *Author's Collection*

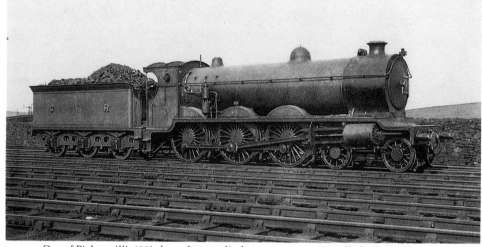

One of Pickersgill's '60' class of two-cylinder 4–6–0s, as originally built for the CR in 1916–1917, a further twenty being added to their number by the LMS in 1925–1926. After the enlargement of the Stranraer turntable, one of these was put on the Glasgow–Stranraer service, but proved unsuccessful and was soon replaced. The type was sluggish and heavy on coal and water. For some reason these engines were known as 'Greybacks', the Scottish term for lice! *Author's Collection*

A British Railways 'Clan' class of light Pacific, 4–6–2, built by BR in 1951–1952, No. 72000 *Clan Buchanan*. One was occasionally used to haul the night sleeper between Carlisle and Stranraer *via* Kilmarnock and Ayr in the final year of steam operation over this line. *Author's Collection*

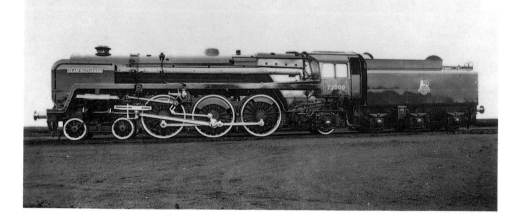

A Glasgow–Stranraer train nearing Pinwherry on 20th July, 1951, headed by Stanier 'Black Five' 4–6–0 No. 45491. Note the 'cut-aways' on the running boards of these engines, to enable them to fit within the loading gauges of all parts of the LMS system.

E.R. Morten

The mid-day train from Glasgow to Stranraer, climbing the bank south of Girvan on 23rd July, 1951, headed by 'Black Five' 4–6–0 No. 44732. *E.R. Morten*

An express from Stranraer headed by LMS 'Crab', 2–6–0 No. 2883, seen here descending the bank from Pinmore in August 1939.   *E.R. Morten*

comfortable fast downhill running, but when they had to tackle steep uphill gradients with such curvature the compounds, in D.L. Smith's phrase, 'had one leg in the air', and this could set the wheels spinning. However, these engines were much appreciated in comparison with the Drummond 4–4–0s, with their vagaries of behaviour.

Good though they were, however, they were in the esteem of the engine crews equalled or bettered by the class '2P' inside-cylindered 4–4–0s which began to work on this line in the autumn of 1928. Here again was a former MR type of locomotive, developed and improved over the years, which had been selected for multiplication in large numbers for passenger duties all over the LMS system. Like Stanier's 'Black Fives' of a later day they could be seen in places as far apart as the far north of Scotland and (by way of the Somerset and Dorset line) the south coast of England. Between 1928 and 1932, 138 were built. They were simple and straightforward in design and resembled the compounds in appearance except in having inside cylinders and being liveried in black instead of red. They were not designed to be greyhounds, though instances of their reaching speeds in the mid-seventies were sometimes noted. They did not, like the Southern Railway's 'L.1' class, which came out shortly before them and were very similar in appearance, have long-travel valves which permitted the quick entrance of steam into the cylinders and its rapid exhaust, but this mattered little on a road where there was no possibility of long-continued high-speed running. What was needed was a reliable machine, able to steam well and having a low appetite for coal and water, and in these respects they gave every satisfaction. The drivers rapidly took to them and referred to them affectionately as the 'wee black yins'. They could run freely even when steam had been shut off, thanks to the 'by-pass' valves in their cylinders which allowed them to 'free-wheel' without having to compress trapped steam with their pistons. Like a cyclist going downhill without pedalling, they could even take short up gradients in their stride. Together with the compounds they predominated on the passenger trains south of Girvan for some years.

In 1935 the first Hughes 2–6–0 'Mogul' began to appear at Stranraer on a daily return trip with the early morning sleeping car boat train from London, which it took over at Carlisle and worked through by way of Dumfries and Newton Stewart. It then had a long wait at Stranraer before returning late in the evening on the corresponding up train, and the following year the decision was made to employ it during this interval on the mid-day train to Glasgow, returning at 3.50 pm from St Enoch. It proved to be most successful on this duty; though officially a mixed traffic engine it could develop a good turn of speed when necessary. More important was its ability to climb banks, in which its adhesion weight, higher than that of any previous engine regularly using this line, could be employed to advantage.

Schedules on the Glasgow–Ayr–Stranraer road had now been quickened, and loads were also on the increase, often topping the 300-ton mark. By now the Midland compounds' performances had somewhat fallen off, partly because of difficulties in maintaining them efficiently, an art that Scottish sheds found difficult. So the drivers on this section were glad to have Moguls available, and did not worry about their appearance, though they looked rather ungainly.

This design was then some 10 years old, the first ones having come into service in 1926. Basically their design was that of George Hughes, the last locomotive superintendent of the Lancashire and Yorkshire Railway and for a brief while chief mechanical engineer of the LMS. Sir Henry Fowler, who succeeded him in 1925, made a few alterations. These engines looked unusual through having the running plates on either side raised exceptionally high above the outside cylinders, the latter being very steeply inclined to the horizontal; this was done on Fowler's instructions in order to bring the engine within the MR loading gauge. They had outside Walschaert's valve gear, which was supported by a long vertical bracket that sometimes fractured in use. A credit point was the fitting of very large and roomy cabs which greatly added to the enginemen's comfort. They were more powerful than any engine previously using this line south of Ayr, but nevertheless they were short enough to fit the 50-foot Stranraer turntable. More of them were soon transferred to work other Stranraer–Glasgow trains.

Three years later the Stranraer turntable was replaced by one large enough to turn a 4–6–0 locomotive, so that it at last became possible to use engines of this size on through services to and from Glasgow. One such type which appeared briefly on this line was W. Pickersgill's class '60', of which he had built six in 1916–1917 for use on the CR. Nine years later the LMS built 20 more, very slightly different in detail, to supplement them. These engines are usually reckoned among Pickersgill's failures, for they were sluggish on the road. Intended as an improvement on McIntosh's inside-cylindered 4–6–0s, they were worse rather than better. In 1939 one of them was put on the Glasgow–Stranraer run. It was not in good condition and consumed vast amounts of water, and it soon vanished when Stanier's 'Black Fives' and 'Jubilees' came to replace it. A couple of years later a few of them returned at a time of engine shortage for working freight trains. Although some drivers managed to get reasonable work out of them, they were nevertheless unpopular with the crews – partly because under wartime conditions maintenance was skimped. They were derisively termed 'Greybacks', possibly because of their unkempt appearance, with a greyish-white mixture of soot and ash adhering to their boiler tops; possibly because that is a common term in Scotland for a louse, and their performances were usually lousy! D.L. Smith cites an amusing example of a driver who had discovered how to handle them to best advantage.

> About this time Jimmy Copeland was on that train. He had only a young passed cleaner with him . . . When they came out for the 6.15 pm [goods train, Stranraer to Glasgow] here was a Greyback waiting for them. The boy nearly fainted. 'Now, now,' said Jimmy, 'don't be getting excited . . . You do as I tell you and we'll not get on so bad.' So he made up the fire himself; then he turned to the water-gauge and put his finger on the half-way position. 'Now', he said to the fireman, 'keep your water level there. Don't let her rise any higher.' They got away and the boy obeyed orders and kept the water at half-glass. The boiler pressure rose, and presently the wash-out plugs began to fizz. The fireman got ready to jump over the side. 'Don't worry' said Jimmy, 'they do that when you work them at half-glass . . . There's nothing wrong.' 'We had a grand trip,' he told me, 'plenty of steam all the way, and she pulled like a good one.'*

---

*D.L. Smith: *Legends of the G&SWR in LMS days*: p. 127.

However, as Smith admitted, this was an exceptional experience, and he had heard 'many grisly tales of the other kind.' After the war these engines were withdrawn, the first going in 1946.

The next 4–6–0 type to appear was the Stanier 'Black Five'. Its manufacture had commenced in 1934 and continued right into BR days, the last order being placed in 1947 on the eve of nationalisation. The days of Midland domination on the LMS had ended, W.A. Stanier having now replaced Sir Henry Fowler as chief mechanical engineer in 1932. He brought with him from Swindon new ideas and practices. The story of the changes he made in locomotive policy, which eventually culminated in the production of the 'Duchess' Pacifics, is familiar and need not be dwelt on here; the design of his which most affected the LMS system was the class '5' two-cylinder mixed traffic 4–6–0, whose numbers eventually reached the huge total of 842. This type proved able to undertake almost any duty successfully, including the haulage of express passenger trains on fast schedules. The first ones to be put to work between Glasgow and Stranraer appeared in April 1939. Their abilities were soon appreciated, but they had one defect, of which D.L. Smith writes amusingly:

> One evening in mid-May I was returning from Stranraer on the 7.13 pm with No. 5319 and the usual three coaches. At New Luce I was bidden to the footplate and given the driver's seat, but not for long. At every revolution of the wheels there came a violent kick in the pants! I rose rather hurriedly – I had never felt anything like it . . . we tried the engine all sorts of ways . . . but we just could not cut out that knock.*

However, it was not until 1942 that the 'Black Fives' were used in any numbers on the Girvan–Stranraer route. During the previous two years another Stanier 4–6–0 type predominated – the class '5X' three-cylinder 'Jubilee'. This type had been built to haul expresses with moderate loads on fast schedules, particularly on the MR main line. They suffered from a number of teething troubles at first, but by 1939 these had been cured and they were operating well on their designated duties when World War II broke out. Services everywhere were then decelerated and passenger traffic became much reduced. However, on the approaches to Stranraer patronage considerably increased because of the large numbers of troops stationed in Ulster as a precautionary measure against enemy landings in Ireland. So in 1940 several '5X' engines were sent to this area to provide adequate locomotive power, their haulage ability rather than their speed capacity being the requirement. They worked the heavier Glasgow–Stranraer services successfully. D.L. Smith was on the footplate of No. 5731 *Perseverance* on 17th August, 1940, at a time when the invasion of Britain by Germany seemed imminent, and described how the engine coped with the 4.20 pm up train from Stranraer.

> I came on the footplate . . . with Jimmy Murray (him they called 'Dungaree'), and Joe Byers firing. We had seven coaches, 211 tons, and they were full. It is strange to look back on that journey. Our country was in direst peril, yet there we were on that glorious day of sunshine, that splendid engine roaring up those hills – 45 per cent cut-off and full regulator, and we were still going more than 30 mph at the

*D.L. Smith: *Legends of the G&SWR in LMS days*: p. 95.

head of the Swan's Neck . . . 60 minutes 7 seconds, that was our running time to Girvan.*

Along with the 'Jubilees' some of the similarly-powered though different-ly-shaped 'Baby Scot' 4–6–0s occasionally showed up on these services. They were Fowler's last design and resembled in appearance the as yet unrebuilt 'Royal Scots', but were a little smaller. They took the places of withdrawn 'Claughtons' in 1930. Their performances matched those of the 'Jubilees' and they were similarly appreciated by their crews.

In 1941 two ghosts from the past materialised at Stranraer, specifically detailed for hauling empty stock to Ayr and back for servicing there. The need to provide adequate transport for service personnel going on or off leave from and to Ulster obliged the provision of an extra return boat service between Stranraer and Larne, and of two trains of enormous length which originated in London and Cardiff respectively. These reached Stranraer in the early morning and returned at 6.30 in the evening. Each had 16 coaches, including a buffet car. Stranraer had the ability to service only one of them in the turn-round period, so the other had to be taken to Ayr, almost 60 miles away. After attempting to use a pair of 0–6–0s to handle this return journey the authorities decided that larger engines were needed. The only ones available at a time of nationwide shortage were two of the 'River' class 4–6–0s of 1915 vintage, once splendid engines with a melancholy history.† They were now temporarily reprieved from the scrap heap and sent to Stranraer, where the men at the shed nicknamed them 'Scharnhorst' and 'Gneisenau' after two German warships which had recently narrowly escaped destruction in an up-Channel dash back to their homeland. These two engines, Nos. 14758 and 14760, always working as a pair, daily hauled the Cardiff leave train to Ayr and back, taking 3 hours each way. Once hostilities had ended they went back to be scrapped.

Once the European war was over there were no changes in locomotive usage between Girvan and Stranraer during the 2½ years that were still to elapse before the railways were brought under state ownership. It was an unhappy period. D.L. Smith speaks of 'wretched timekeeping, engines in vile order, bad coal, shortage of steam, no heat in the trains, coaches worn and draughty – but no crowding; people were deserting the trains for the buses.' Under BR things were slowly to improve, and within 20 years steam was to disappear from the scene altogether.

In 1951 one of the new range of standard locomotive types began to appear on the line south of Girvan – the new class '5' 4–6–0. In many ways it was similar to the Stanier 'Black Five', but dimensionally was slightly larger and had coupled wheels 2 inches larger in diameter. It was put on the Glasgow –Stranraer services, both passenger and freight. Others followed. Unfortu-nately the crews did not take to them and preferred the 'Black Fives'. It is

---

*D.L. Smith: Legends of the G&SWR in LMS days: pp. 94–95.

---

†The 'Rivers' were designed in 1915 by F.G. Smith, locomotive superintendent on the Highland Railway, and when they appeared they were, outside the GWR, the most advanced passenger locomotives in regard to design on any British railway. Unfortunately they were heavier than expected, and a dispute over their use arose between Smith and the HR's Chief Engineer, which ended in Smith being told to resign. The engines were then sold to the CR, in whose service they gave every satisfaction. In LMS years they were used on the HR main line and, it was found, did the track no damage at all – probably because, though heavy, they had their working parts extremely well balanced and inflicted very little hammer-blow.

since only a few years later the decision was taken to phase out steam altogether and build diesel-powered engines for use everywhere except on the electrified lines.

Finally one must mention the standard 4–6–2s, the 'Clans' and 'Britannias' which, shortly before their withdrawal, operated between Ayr and Stranraer on the re-routed sleeping car trains from and to London, and on the daytime trains between Stranraer and Newcastle-on-Tyne; these had previously used the now-closed direct route between Dumfries and Stranraer. These were the heaviest and most powerful engines that ever worked on the line south of Girvan. The night sleepers from and to London, that connected with the early morning and late evening boats, loaded very heavily, and the authorities evidently did not trust the abilities of any other available type. Indeed, south of Ayr they arranged for both the 'Clans' and 'Britannias' to be piloted by a class '5' engine so that there should be no stalling on any of the banks.

The 4–6–2s in question were shedded at Kingmoor, Carlisle, and each one rostered for this service made the return trip by way of Dumfries, Mauchline and Ayr, going out in the early morning and returning late at night. One would like to have evidence of how well they coped with these last duties before being withdrawn in 1966. Manned by crews who were used to working them, they presumably performed satisfactorily, and on fairly leisurely timings would seldom have needed to be extended, especially when piloted, but there must have been occasions when late starts obliged forceful running. However, few of the passengers would have been interested in taking records late at night or early in the morning; most would have been settling down to sleep or waking with a yawn. Thus the reign of steam ended on the Girvan–Stranraer line – if not with a bang, certainly not with a whimper.

Chapter Nine
Accidents and Mishaps

No serious accident, such as a crash or derailment, has befallen any passenger train on the Girvan–Stranraer line since its construction, though there have been some mishaps, three being serious enough to be mentioned. Each was occasioned by a snowfall.

The first occurred on the evening of 6th February, 1895, when a great storm blew up which affected the whole of Galloway, snow falling thickly and drifting before a south-east wind. Services on the neighbouring Portpatrick & Wigtownshire Joint Committee's lines were badly disorganised, one train being held up for three days near Creetown. The Girvan line was less seriously affected, but the 4.15 pm from Stranraer to Glasgow was unlucky; it managed to struggle as far as a point near Chirmorie summit, but then stuck fast. The engine was 0–6–0 No. 305, formerly No. 7 of the Ayrshire and Wigtownshire, built eight years earlier; the train was made up of four-wheeled coaches. Driver, fireman, guard and passengers were forced to spend the night inside the coaches; when daylight returned they made their way with great difficulty across the snow-covered moors to find shelter in the few houses in the neighbourhood. It was a full week before the train could be extricated and the line re-opened.

Nearly 14 years later, on 28th December, 1908, a similar but worse hold-up happened to a southbound train, the 4.15 pm from Glasgow to Stranraer. The weather was exceedingly cold, but snow did not begin to fall till after mid-day. Six hours later it lay thick on the ground and was beginning to drift. Arriving at Girvan station, the 4.15 exchanged its locomotive for No. 126, one of Smellie's 'Wee Bogie' 4–4–0s, and then waited for the evening train to arrive from Stranraer before it could proceed. The latter arrived late, having battled with the worsening storm all the way, and its driver advised that the southbound service should be cancelled. Nevertheless the risk was taken of letting it proceed. It got through Pinmore tunnel, reached Pinwherry and then Barrhill. Here it was known that the line was drifting up, and many men were out trying to clear the snow, but again there was no attempt to halt the train at the last possible place where food and shelter could have been had. The engine re-started and headed out straight into the wild moorland, up the 1 in 67 gradient, through several deep cuttings which were beginning to fill up with snow. A little over a mile from Barrhill it stuck, set back, charged the drift and got through. A mile further on it stuck again, also in a cutting, and this time it was not able to set back to take a run at the drift. The fireman trudged the two miles back to Barrhill, reported what had happened, gave up his tablet and returned to the train.

At this stage there was some hope that a light engine, which was waiting at Barrhill and in steam, would be able to reach the train and either push it over the summit to a point where the line was passable, or else draw it back to Barrhill. The crew and passengers waited in hope, but the engine never came, for it too got stuck in a drift and had to be abandoned. As the night wore on the snow began to seep through the cracks round the compartment doors, eventually reaching knee-height. There was no steam-heating in the compartments, which got colder and colder. Daylight arrived to find everyone hungry, thirsty and freezing. Two hours after dawn a rescue party arrived from Barrhill, bringing much-needed provisions. So snowed-up were the coaches that the only way to get these to the passengers was to open the lamp-holes in the roofs and lower them down. What could not yet be managed was the victims' extrication, for the sides of the cutting were filled with snow which prevented access to the doors. During the day the water in the locomotive's tender gave out, so that it was no longer safe to have a fire in the firebox; the hot coals were raked out and thrown on the side of the track, and the crew then left the footplate and found shelter in a lineside hut at one end of the cutting. Attempts were made during the day to get a snow-plough through, but despite the efforts of as many as seven engines pushing it, it could reach no further than a mile from the stranded train, the plough then becoming derailed on a curve.

Another horrible night followed for the passengers, who had food but no heating. The next day valiant and ultimately successful attempts were made to clear the doors along one side of the coaches. Meanwhile a relief train made its way as far as it could. The passengers were escorted to it and taken back to Barrhill, there to be lodged for the night. The following day they were conveyed to their homes by one route or another: those bound for Stranraer had to travel by way of Ayr, Kilmarnock and Dumfries, a 190-mile journey to reach a place less than 20 miles away. One of these latter persons died the following day from the privations she had endured.

Not quite so dreadful, but bad enough, was a similar event nearly 40 years later, during the terrible winter of 1947, when the 5.10 pm from Glasgow, headed by a 'Jubilee' 4–6–0, No. 5728, *Defiance*, and manned by a Stranraer crew, set out from Girvan on time with a light load of four corridor coaches carrying 57 passengers. Even as late as their departure from Glasgow there had been no indication that almost the worst snowstorm on record in Galloway was about to break out; it had been bitterly cold for seven weeks, but England had had it worse, and on 12th March one was within sight of spring. Nevertheless at about dusk the snow and wind came together, and a howling blizzard soon covered the whole area.

The train reached Glenwhilly on time, but was then held up to pass the evening freight train from Stranraer, which had already left New Luce. After an 80 minutes' wait word came back that the northbound train was unable to get through and had returned to New Luce. It was now necessary to send for a snow-plough; one arrived at 11 pm and continued south to New Luce. Going slowly, as was unavoidable when the track had to be cleared, it passed the end of the section after midnight, and the 5.10 pm from Glasgow resumed its journey.

Unfortunately the track cleared by the plough had been rapidly filling up again, and *Defiance*, despite its light load, could only get as far as the top of the hump half a mile south of Glenwhilly; then it stuck in the cutting. The fireman made his way back to Glenwhilly and reported what had happened. Had the train been able to follow close behind the snow-plough and its engine it could without doubt have been able to get through, but the hour's delay had given the snow time again to accumulate. In the darkness it would have been difficult, though possible, to get the passengers out of the train and back down the line to Glenwhilly. As the train had both light from the coach batteries and several packages of food in the guard's van intended for canteens in the Stranraer area, it seemed better not to attempt an escape. The passengers therefore ate what they needed and settled down for the night. It was not so far promising to be so fearsome an ordeal, for the driver and fireman remained on the footplate and kept the fire going, so that steam could get through to the heaters in the coaches.

The following day the weather was as bad as ever. Fortunately they were near enough to Glenwhilly for people there to send up relays of hot tea. So far the passengers' experience had been nothing like as unpleasant as in 1908, for they could communicate with one another or reach the toilet compartment along the corridor, and they had been kept warm. However, at mid-day the tender tank became empty and the fire had to be removed from the firebox, so that there was no more steam heating. Outside it became colder and continued to snow. Such was the pressure of the latter on the windward side of the train that some of the large plate-glass windows cracked, and one broke, injuring two passengers. The lights in the coaches flickered and went out as the batteries became exhausted. The second night was far worse than the first. Meanwhile attempts were being made to get a snowplough through, but they failed.

During the night the storm blew itself out and the snow stopped falling. Once daylight had come it was safe to leave the train, and the passengers were guided down to Glenwhilly and given shelter in near-by houses, where roaring fires were built up to warm them, coal being fetched from the locomotive's tender by volunteer sledge parties. In the evening a relief train from Stranraer was able to reach a point some three miles away, on the Swan's Neck, and those who were fit to make the journey were escorted down to it and managed to reach Stranraer that evening. The others had to wait till the following day, when another train got within easy walking distance of Glenwhilly, and a relief party from it, of police and German prisoners awaiting repatriation, took the remaining passengers, many on stretchers, down to board it. It was another two days before the engine and coaches could be dug out of the snow and hauled down to Stranraer.

Comparing the 1908 and 1947 incidents, one notes how improvements in rail transport mitigated hardships which might earlier have led to tragedy. On the latter occasion there were lights and heating in the train for half the time that it was stranded. Corridors alongside the compartments permitted passengers to keep in touch with each other. There were almost enough upholstered seats in the train to permit everyone to lie down during the night. The absence of compartment doors prevented snow from getting into the compartments, except into the one where the window had been broken. It was not necessary to clear the whole of one side of the train to set passengers free, as they could walk to the rear end of the train through the vestibules. On the other hand, it was easier for the pressure of the snow to break the larger windows of the coaches; smaller ones would have withstood the strain better.

As against the three snowstorm incidents, in which passenger trains were involved, the Girvan–Stranraer line experienced only two accidents. These both involved freight trains, in which damage was done to vehicles, though there were several other less serious mishaps, many of which are enter-

tainingly described in David L. Smith's book from which I have quoted in
the previous chapter. On 15th November, 1922 a southbound freight train
suffered a very unusual misfortune. Most goods trains on all lines then, and
for a long while afterwards, did not have continuous braking. This meant
that on a heavily-graded road, since it was not possible to run the whole time
with taut couplings, the rear vehicles of a goods train, after passing a summit
and going on to a steep down gradient, would tend to press forward against
their buffers and the couplings would go slack. If the latter were suddenly
tightened by a tug from the engine one might snap under the strain. In this
particular instance the night freight train from Glasgow to Stranraer, headed
by two Manson 0–6–0s Nos. 173 and 185, had surmounted the summit
north of Pinmore tunnel at about 5.30 am when the first of two coupling
breakages occurred. The train crew had been informed that there was a cattle
wagon to be attached to their train at Pinwherry, and the driver of the front
engine, confusing Pinwherry with Pinmore, braked as he approached the
latter station, preparing to stop. When his fireman pointed out the mistake
he released the brakes, the train then travelling at about 15 mph. The jolt
caused the doupling between the two engines to snap, and it was necessary
to stop to replace it by that of the other engine.

This having been done, they re-started, and the sudden tightening of
coupling links throughout the train caused the one between the fourth and
fifth wagons to snap. They were on a down gradient, and while the rear of
the train went forward by gravity, slightly impeded by the fact that the guard
had his van brakes on, it was not at first evident that a detachment had
occurred. However, the two portions now began gradually to draw apart,
and this at length became apparent to the locomotive crews when, looking
back on a curve, they saw the reflection of the light in the guard's van against
the side of the cutting further back than it should have been.

In order to lessen the impact when the rear part of the train hit the front
part, as was now bound to happen, the driver of the second engine opened
his regulator. The engine now began to prime and steam failed to reach the
cylinders, so there was no acceleration. The collision therefore occurred
forcefully, resulting in a great pile-up of wagons that reached to the top of
the cutting through which the train had been travelling. There was much
material damage, but fortunately no one was injured. At the subsequent
enquiry it was established that the broken wagon-coupling had developed a
flaw, possibly due to metal-fatigue. The whole incident was an example of
the dangers inherent in running freight trains over steep gradients without
continuous braking.

On 22nd July, 1928, at a point not far from the earlier accident, the
6.35 pm freight train from Stranraer to Glasgow was de-railed just north of
Pinwherry in circumstances which at the time could find no explanation.
The train had stopped at Barrhill for a long while to allow the 5.10 pm from
Glasgow to pass it. Up to this point the driver, who was new to the road, had
been meticulously careful. From Barrhill the line goes steeply down to
Pinwherry, and with this train it was usual, once it had started, to let it coast
and apply the brakes on approaching Pinwherry at the bottom of the dip in
order to slow down for the reverse curves through the loop, after which the

regulator would be opened again. The engine on this occasion was No. 17759, a Drummond 'Pumper'. The load was one wagon short of the maximum for this type of locomotive over this road. Both the guard's van and the vehicle next to the engine had brakes.

Everything went normally until within sight of the distant signal at the approach to Pinwherry. Then the locomotive began a long continuous whistle, which alerted everyone at the station. The permitted speed through the latter was 15 mph, since two reverse curves had to be taken, but the train came through between the platforms at a much higher speed, the whistling stopping as it reached the signal box. The engine rocked wildly over the exit from the loop, proceeded a few yards further beneath the road bridge just north of the station, and then plunged to the left into a meadow beside the track, overturning as it did so. The vehicles piled up behind it. The coupled wheels of the engine continued to revolve for several minutes, showing that the regulator had either been left open or re-opened. Both driver and fireman were killed instantly. The guard, though badly shocked, was unhurt and able to give evidence at the subsequent enquiry, which was held at Pinwherry 10 days later.

The latter's findings were that the driver must have been in error and had forgotten the need to slow down, his unfamiliarity with the road having made him misjudge his speed. It was easy enough to blame a dead man for an inexplicable accident, but what also went unexplained was the long-continued whistling. D.L. Smith could not believe that the driver, whom he personally knew, could have been so careless, and came to the conclusion that the clue to the answer lay in the whistling. There had, he surmised, been occasion to sound the whistle, and it must have stuck open.

Drummond whistles quite often did that. The spindle was high up, near the roof of the cab, so the driver jumped up on his seat box to try to stop the whistle; the fireman probably jumped up too. The two exasperated men struggled with the wretched thing while it squalled on, alarming the whole countryside. When they got it stopped, or maybe before, Robson [the driver] got down, to find that he was well past the accustomed braking point, and that the speed had got much higher than in previous runs . . . There was some sort of speed restriction at Pinwherry, but nobody had told him it was as severe as 15 mph. Pinwherry was in a dip. He had been taught to go fast through a dip to keep the couplings tight, so he let her go, feeling no apprehension. The tablet was exchanged and taken in; as he passed through the station Robson opened his regulator for the ensuing up grade . . . That, I believe, is what happened.*

---

*D.L. Smith: *Legends of the G&SWR in LMS days*: pp. 44–45.

Chapter Ten
A Fireman's Memories

Bob Smillie, recently retired from his post as a driver on British Rail, whose home town and base was Ayr, has kindly contributed some memories of his own, dating from the days of steam beginning in 1944, when he was first a cleaner, then a fireman, during the last days of the LMS and the early years of BR. In his belief the route from Ayr to Stranraer is one of the most difficult in Britain, and by those footplatemen who were only occasionally asked to take a train along it, it was regarded, to use his own words, with a mixture of 'dread, challenge and apprehension.' Whereas from Glasgow to Ayr all was plain sailing on almost level track, from Ayr to Stranraer it was a switch-back of steep rises and falls, with some pitches as severe as 1 in 60, while beyond Girvan it was single track with even steeper gradients and a start from the water column at Girvan at 1 in 50 for a short distance.

Bob's first firing turn came during 1945, when he was sent as a passenger to Stranraer to work a light engine back thence to Ayr, with a well-known driver on that route, Jimmy Cairns. It was then that he got his first 'feel' of the road, and learned the importance of using his ears to detect sounds from the passage of the engine over the track, so that he knew where he was on what might be a pitch-black night, and similarly using his eyes during the daytime, to notice landmarks such as streams, clumps of trees or permanent way lineside huts, when they were visible. His second firing turn was with a Fowler 'Mogul', No. 2808, with John MacCallum, 'a very tall, well-built man with bright red hair, well and truly trained in the hard, wild days of the old "Sou-West".' They were to take the engine light to Stranraer shed and leave it there. Bob remembers firing diligently all the way from Ayr to the entrance of Pinmore tunnel, when MacCallum told him to put his shovel down. 'It's doonhill fur a lang while noo. D'ye no ken the road at a'? Bring over the tablet and I'll show ye how tae change it at Pinmore Box.'

Once he had graduated from 'passed cleaner' to fireman, Bob had plenty of opportunity to 'learn the road', particularly with freight trains.

With the exception of a few miles, it is either pounding hard uphill or hanging on like grim death downhill, brakes galore, using judgement and hoping for good luck as well. Southbound it was at 1 in 50 off the platform after taking water from the column at the south end of Girvan station. Then the battle began, with a grind up through Glendoune cutting, on curves. If you made it past the waterworks, between overbridges 13 and 14, you were safely on your way. From Pinmore tunnel it was downhill all the way to Pinwherry. Then the real test started in earnest, with a long section to Barrhill followed by a longer one to Glenwhilly. Tablets were changed at the best possible speeds to enable one to get over the top. For many miles now it was through a wild and barren landscape with much curvature, up to a very brief level bit, and then the final 1 in 124 to Chirmorie summit near some now disused permanent-way workers' cottages. At one time there was a small platform here, where twice a week (I think) supplies were left and members of families were picked up or set down. After the summit the line fell steeply to Glenwhilly, where one changed the tablet and then set off up the short but tough stretch at 1 in 77 to the place where the old 5.10 from Glasgow once got stuck [as described in the previous chapter]. Then followed the descent down the 1 in 57/58 grades round the Swan's Neck, where speed is restricted to 40 mph, and across the Luce Water viaduct into the loop at New Luce.

After this point there are ups and downs on moderate grades. Starting very gently from New Luce, one either coasted along or gingerly kept the regulator open to get a breath of steam, with the guard meanwhile slightly applying his handbrake to keep all the couplings tight. There were two crossings to watch for, at Airy-holland and Craig, named after farms close to the railway, where there were crossing keepers but no signals. Then one went over a slight hump to approach the signal at Challoch Junction. Formerly there had been a signal box here, but in my early days the points were, as they are now, controlled from the next box at Dunragit. Just before Challoch Junction there was a sand-drag which diverged to the north-west, to protect the junction in case a south-coming train from Girvan misjudged its speed and passed the signal when the latter was at 'danger'.

Bob remembered one occasion when he was firing on a locomotive which did exactly this.

Driver John Vallance, on ex-CR No. 17628, with a load of empty cattle wagons, misjudged his speed over the hump north of the Junction, and saw the signal ahead of him was red. He ran past it and entered the sand drag, but luckily did not go very far and was not really de-railed. After he had assessed the situation he decided to try and shove back. His experienced guard, 'Fiddler' Aitchison, knew what was taking place and eased the brakes. As we were doing this we heard the roar of a train making its way east to Glenluce on the Port line, and it was quite an experience to see and hear the different chimney beats from '4P' compound No. 1179 and the six-beat '5XP' No. 5657, Tyrwhitt. The look on both drivers' faces, who were heading a special troop train, was one of sheer bewilderment.

He remembers the two CR, ex-HR, 4–6–0s, which were used during the war to haul an empty stock train of great length, as mentioned above in Chapter 8, and showed me a water-colour painting of one of them, done by a fellow-driver, Sam Crooks, of Ayr shed.

Two of them were based at Ayr around 1944–1945, which were numbered 14758 and 14760. My own experience with them was on what were called 'trip shunting turns', when one started from Falkland Junction and shunted at every yard to Kilwinning. They were big brutes, with a 'room and kitchen' firebox, though the latter was not very deep, which was a blessing for those who had to clean them out often. I heard many accounts of the working of these engines. Their tenders were very large, and they had steam reversers, which were not liked by the footplate men, because one could never be sure that they would actually function. They had rather unusual injectors, which were certainly efficient; they could be set at a minimum feed, and drivers told me about putting them on and keeping them on for most of the journey.

He remembers particularly the 'banking jobs'.

Ayr had duties where banking was done from Girvan to an official point known as 'OB [overbridge] 16'. At this point the banking engine is nearly but not quite at the top of the gradient. It was an interesting operating event. A special banking key was given by the signalman at Girvan No. 2 box to the rear driver. The banker came against the brake van buffers at the rear, and when the train was ready to depart and the signals had come off, and the leading driver was in possession of a token either to Pinmore or to Pinwherry, and the banking driver had his special key, the guard hand-signalled the banking driver, who gave two cock-crow whistles; a hand signal was then given to the leading driver, who repeated the same code on his own whistle. Both engines then steamed away together. There was a rule that if for any reason the banker lost contact with the brake van buffers he was not allowed to catch up again. What in practice actually happened may be best left to the imagination, since in such a case the front engine was certain to stick anyhow. At No. 16 bridge the banker would normally give a 'cheerio' whistle, and reverse and return to Girvan; the train by this time would have entered the tunnel and be ready to descend on 1 in 92. But there were some wild men about! Trained in the hardy times of the G & SWR, many would keep on steaming from the rear further than was laid down, on the basis of, 'we'll make sure he doesn't stick before that tunnel.' One could almost hear the shouts and curses of the front enginemen, who were now concerned about the drop towards Pinmore – for most trains were entirely loose-coupled, with brakes only on the engine and the brake van (unless the wagon brakes were also pinned down) and the falling gradients went right through to Pinwherry.

Coal was a problem at this time, during the immediate post-war years.

It was often of the poorest quality. The best was kept for the long-distance passenger work – e.g. Glasgow to London. Stranraer seemed always to get coal with a very high sulphur content. This was no great problem until one reached the bore of the single-line tunnel at Pinmore. Pulling heavily from the level at Pinwherry station up the severe grades beyond (especially if the rails were bad between Pinmore station and the tunnel entrance) brought the speed down, and bad slipping would occur inside the tunnel itself, even though it was considered to be the driest on the whole of the old South Western system. It was then that the sulphur caused havoc. Men were choked by the fumes, and the slower the speed, the worse the problem was. It became rather frightening; you could not get your breath and there was much spluttering. My first bout of this quite scared me, but Sammy Taylor, my driver at the time, demonstrated how to overcome the menace. He shouted across the footplate, 'Get yer hanky, Bobby. Soak it in that pail of water.' (Water that was none too clean, as it happened.) 'Hold it across yer nose and mouth.' Here was another old-fashioned G & SWR trick I was being introduced to. Anyway, it certainly helped.

Finally, the experiences and problems on 'assisting turns' on the night goods train between College Yard, Glasgow, and Stranraer. From Ayr onwards it was frequently the case that pilot assistance was judged to be necessary, and any spare locomotive which was in steam might be selected for that purpose, a crew being told off to drive and fire it. After this particular turn the train engine crews would be lodged at Stranraer, where the lodging arrangements and the food provided were reckoned to be the best on the system. But the pilot crews which assisted the 1 am were not supposed to go as far as Stranraer, except when it was really unavoidably necessary, but had to return from New Luce, at which point the work on the heavy grades was all over and the train engine could fend for itself. Coming back from New Luce, tender-first, was all very well in good weather, but in wintry conditions, without the shelter of the front of the cab, it could be thoroughly uncomfortable, and the men on the pilot engine were wont to employ every ruse and stratagem which they could think of to justify continuing to Stranraer and taking their share of its comforts and culinary delights before turning on the turntable and coming back. Bob Smillie recalls some of the brushes with authority which followed these unauthorised prolongations of piloting.

Water was taken for this turn at Girvan goods station, where detachments were often made; then one went on 'up the hill'. The arrangement for the pilot engine on this turn was to 'tie off' at New Luce and return light, tender first, either all the way to Ayr or, if you wanted to, going into the old locomotive shed at Girvan and turning there on the table. More rows broke out at Ayr depot between the management and the crews over this duty than over anything else. When crews booked on the foreman would very firmly remind the drivers of the pilot engines: 'Now, remember you come off at New Luce'; or, 'On no account do you go on to Stranraer.' But in bad weather what actually happened was another story. It was then an unpleasant job, with both engines battering away uphill and holding on downhill, with the steaming of either engine dependent on so many factors such as bad coal, dirty boiler tubes, blast-pipes maybe out of proper alignment – there were so many reasons why things could go wrong.

Often one of the two crews would unjustly accuse the other of not pulling their weight, and sometimes, of course, it did give an excuse for 'taking it a wee bit easy', but the weight of the trains, bad rail conditions or stormy weather did mean that unless you blasted hell out of the engines you simply did not arrive at the signal box at the end of each section. On bitter winter nights some men would just refuse to uncouple at New Luce, and the signalman would be given some reason such as, 'The rear engine is in bother', 'We need a fitter at Stranraer' or 'It'll be quicker for us to get back, rather than detaching here and waiting.' Behind all this was the ploy to get right through for comfort, being able to turn at Stranraer, perhaps get some better coal, fill up the tank and get right away to Ayr. And in actual fact it did prove most of the time that one could get back home as early doing this. But there were occasions when that didn't work out, and overtime was incurred – and overtime itself was a factor with some drivers who wanted to make an extra shilling.

And so there would be verbal exchanges after they had returned to Ayr. The day shift foreman would want to know why the crew had not obeyed the instructions of the night shift foreman, and would possibly report the matter to the shed master.

The attitude of the men was that, considering the shortage of 'Storm sheets' (which came across the space between the cab and the tender to give partial protection to the crew) they had every justification for avoiding the 'tie off' at New Luce. Many stood firm on this issue, and eventually the Control Centre at Kilmarnock became involved, and definitely instructed the New Luce signalman to keep his starting signal at danger and not issue a fresh tablet. The driver and fireman of the pilot engine would then often have words with the unfortunate signalman, and choice language, not repeated here, would follow over the 'phone between the driver and the Controller. All too often the consequence was a tender-first return to Girvan, sometimes in freezing cold weather, and both men having a restricted view along the tender sides, making it awkward to look out for anyone on the track, or any obstruction. There was no respite.

Such were the troubles and trials of locomotive crews working freight trains over this difficult stretch of line during the days of steam. With the passing of the steam locomotive and its replacement by diesel traction things became easier, and perhaps less interesting as material for the raconteur. The comradeship of the footplate gave place to the solitary driver on his seat in the driving compartment. The privations disappeared, but the need for vigilance remained.

Chapter Eleven
The Line Since 1965

The last three decades on the Girvan–Stranraer line since the demise of steam have seen a number of changes and ended with a large question mark looming over the line's future. Passenger and freight services still operate, and in some respects the former are better than they ever have been. However, the provision of relatively cheap flights on a good air service between Glasgow and Belfast has had as one consequence the transference of custom from rail to air by that great stand-by of railway trunk routes, the business man, who always prefers to take the quickest way to his destination. A journey time between those two cities of less than an hour contrasts with six hours or more by rail and conventional steamer, with, nowadays, no provision of first class accommodation. Moreover, with one exception (mentioned later in this chapter) there is no longer the degree of co-ordination between the railway and the cross-channel ferries which used to exist; the latter are now organised principally for the benefit of the motorist and lorry-driver, so that most of the waits between the trains and the boats are long ones.

It would therefore be not at all surprising if the whole line between Ayr and Stranraer were soon to be closed, as happened to the Stranraer–Dumfries line. This would be a lamentable thing, but the days are now almost past when a railway's duty was to provide a public service rather than profits for shareholders. Environmental considerations certainly favour the encouragement of the railway and the discouragement of petrol- or diesel-driven vehicles, but money talks louder than green issues, and until we begin to choke in the fumes we emit it will no doubt go on doing so. Perhaps, therefore, the days of the interesting little railway which is the subject of this book are numbered. In that event the latter will have to be thought of as an obituary rather than an appreciation. Time will tell.

The choice of Dr Richard Beeching for the Chairmanship of the British Railways Board, and the drastic excision of non-profit-making services which he proposed in his Report, and which was in large measure carried out, has often been described and discussed, in praise or blame. All that one needs to remark here is that initially the closures of 1965 resulted in more, not fewer trains running on the Girvan–Stranraer line. Previously the traffic from and to England had gone by way of the direct route between Carlisle and Stranraer through Castle Douglas, but after this was closed passengers had to make a wide detour, going north-west from Dumfries along the former G & SWR main line, turning west at Mauchline over a branch through Annbank Junction to Ayr, and thence proceeding south. The distance was some 45 miles further, and was to be increased still more at a later date when the diversion was extended to include Kilmarnock and Troon. So for some while extra trains used the Girvan–Stranraer line – the night sleeping car service from London in particular.

Although the line itself remained open, all but one of the stations south of Girvan were closed. These included the former Town station at Stranraer, so that the Harbour station on the quayside now became the terminus for all trains. Barrhill alone was spared, largely because of vigorous pressure for its retention by the railway unions, and it is now a convenient place for making road connections to and from Newton Stewart and the Machars. The removal of its sidings has left room for a small car park. The platforms at other stations were removed and the buildings dismantled or disposed of. Except at Glenwhilly and Barrhill all crossing loops were dismantled; the one at Glenwhilly has now also gone, being removed in 1992. Semaphore signalling remained, with single line block working and hand tablet exchange.

From the middle of 1965 the services between Glasgow and Stranraer settled down to four each way daily, with one on Sundays, to which one or two were added during the summer months. These continued to be operated by multiple unit trains, except between 1984 and 1987, when locomotive-hauled stock was used again. Between Girvan and Stranraer only one stop was made, at Barrhill. So these 38 miles took less time than before, the 64-minute allowance, including the halt at Barrhill, coming down in 1973 to between 57 and 60 minutes; a contributory reason for this was of course the absence of the necessity to slow to exchange tablets at what had now ceased to be passing loops. In 1977 there was some deceleration, 68 minutes now becoming the usual time taken; with occasional exceptions this became the rule in the southbound direction for a while, though the northbound service was gradually speeded up again until in 1982 most trains took about an hour. From 1984 the southbound trains were quickened to match. Sunday trains ran in much the same timings as the weekday ones.

Until August 1967 the weekend trains, which had formerly used the direct route from Newcastle-on-Tyne through Carlisle, Dumfries and Newton Stewart in connection with the boat services, continued to run on the new route, both day and night. During 1967–1968 this service was suspended; then it came back for a couple of years; then for a further three years it operated only in the daytime; then it was suspended once more. During 1977–1978 a down day and a night up train appeared, but only between Stranraer and Carlisle where connections were made with other services to or from Newcastle or the south. The following year this service was increased to provide day and night journeys in both directions, the daytime trains running every weekday. In 1981 these latter blossomed out as a through service to and from Euston, the 'Northern Irishman', and this continued until 1988. All were locomotive-hauled, and after the extension of the daytime service to London buffet facilities were provided. Since their loads were much heavier than those of the Glasgow trains they had rather slower timings between Girvan and Stranraer.

The through night sleeper trains from and to Euston, which had previously gone by way of Castle Douglas, took the new longer route from June 1965. At first it was a fairly heavy train and, as mentioned in Chapter 7, required for a year or so the services of a 'Clan' or 'Britannia' 4–6–2, with additional assistance south of Ayr. In those days the train included at least two sleeping cars, one for each class of passenger; they were of the Mark I type, the second class compartments each having two berths, the first class only one. At busy periods this service could load to over 450 tons and perhaps include three sleepers. In either direction it was used by passengers from or to Ayr, who much appreciated this first direct link with the English capital. At Girvan, too, a demand arose that the train should be timetabled to stop there (which, unofficially, it usually did) and this was acceded to. Patronage, however, was to fall off later.

Class '47' No. 47447 arriving at Girvan on 3rd November, 1984 with the 11.30 pm Stranraer to Glasgow service.

Tom Heavyside

The main arrival and departure platform at Stranraer station, looking towards Girvan.
Author

Barrhill station in May 1992 showing the station building (with clock) still on active service on the down platform. *Author*

An earlier view in November, 1984 of Barrhill station (at that time white-washed) with the driver of class '47' No. 47447 about to pick up the tablet from the signalman.

Tom Heavyside

The up platform (No. 1) at Barrhill station, May 1992.   *Author*

The 11.53 am service from Glasgow to Stranraer about to change tablets at Glenwhilly station in July 1992.   *Author*

The 11.53 am four-coach Super-Sprinter from Glasgow to Stranraer halting at Girvan, May 1989.   *Author*

The 11.53 am four-coach Super-Sprinter (same set as above) waits to depart from platform 9, Glasgow Central station, for Stranraer, in August 1990. Note the diminutive snow plough (which has never yet been needed) and the central buffing/coupling gear.   *Author*

Class '47' No. 47016 arriving at Stranraer on a seven-coach 'Sealink' service from Glasgow on 2nd November, 1984.　　　*Tom Heavyside*

Glenwhilly signal box, July 1992.
Author

Barrhill signal cabin. This was originally erected at Portpatrick but later
removed in 1935 to Barrhill as a replacement for the fire damaged signal
box there. Portpatrick no longer needed
the box as its branch was being worked
on the 'one engine in steam' principle.
Author

A final view of the refurbished Stranraer station in November 1984 with class '47' No. 47016 on the service from Glasgow. *Tom Heavyside*

The night sleeper trains were at first worked by way of Annbank Junction but were later routed through Kilmarnock and Troon. After 1966 they were diesel-hauled north and west of Carlisle. Because of the gradients and heavier loadings the timings over the Girvan–Stranraer section were easier than for the Glasgow trains. In later years, when loads had decreased, they became through portions attached to other trains or detached from them, not always at the same place. I travelled on the up service on one occasion in a sleeping compartment. We left Stranraer at the usual time; waking up during the night, I got up and looked out of the window, to find that we were standing at Carstairs, for the through London portion no longer ran by way of Kilmarnock and Dumfries, as I had supposed, but was going right into Glasgow, reversing out along the West Coast main line and joining the Fort William train at some suitable spot (it may have been Carstairs) along it. It was a sign of the decreased custom on this train that it only had one sleeping car, and that I had a two-berth compartment to myself. According to the timetable it ran for the last time on 1st October, 1989; in fact it continued to run unadvertised for another year.

The locomotives used on the through trains to London or Newcastle were of course standard BR diesel-electric types, either class '27', '37' or '47'. A '37' was powerful enough to cope with a load of up to six coaches, and a '47' could manage the night sleeper unaided, having 2,750 hp at its disposal. My friend Ross Cunningham, of Portpatrick, who has had frequent cause to use the line during the period now under review, recorded a number of runs on the Girvan–Stranraer section which show commendable efforts on the part of drivers to regain lost time. For example, on 12th October, 1977 the 11 am from Stranraer, with a class '47' and five coaches, left the Harbour station 32 minutes late and had recovered 17 of them by the time Girvan was reached, taking 33 minutes to Barrhill and a further 15 onwards. On Christmas Eve 1979 No. 47485 took eight bogie vehicles on the 10.35 am and reached Girvan in 54 minutes, inclusive of the Barrhill stop. In the opposite direction, on 14th October, 1977, another class '47' with a five-coach load reached Stranraer in 58 minutes from Girvan despite a 3-minute halt at Glenwhilly as well as the usual stop at Barrhill.

The rolling stock used when the diesel multiple units ran the Glasgow services were generally three-coach rakes of Swindon build, used singly or in pairs. In 1984, when locomotive haulage for a time replaced the multiple units, special trains were used to connect with the Sealink ferries; they were colourfully, not to say gaudily liveried in red, white and blue with the word 'SEALINK' prominent on each coach side, and somewhat resembled the present Network SouthEast colours which delight some and which others deplore. These trains remained until the coming of the Super Sprinters, described below.

In regard to freight traffic, one may mention the special trains run for Stockton Haulage Ltd, which firm opened a depot on Stranraer Pier in 1976, to which loads of steel destined for Ireland were taken by rail from Stockton-on-Tees and then transferred to lorries with trailers, which were then driven on to the ferry boats and distributed throughout Ulster by road haulage. This venture was partly Government-funded and much was hoped from it, as contemporary local newspapers show. It still operates, but there are fears that it may be entirely transferred to road haulage on this side of the North Channel as well, and thus clog up still further the already-overloaded A75 road along the Solway coast. One hopes these apprehensions will not become actualities, for the loss of this traffic might well tilt the balance towards the eventual closure of the line.

On 3rd October, 1988 the present passenger service was inaugurated, using Super Sprinter diesel multiple units. These provide a quite different standard of service from before, and in the writer's opinion show a distinct improvement in speed, comfort and quality of ride. Timings between Girvan and Stranraer have now been cut to between 55 and 57 minutes in the southbound direction and between 51 to 56 minutes northbound – an indication of the greater power per coach which these units possess. Between Glasgow and Stranraer the overall schedules vary between 2 hours 8 minutes and 2 hours 15 minutes on the through services, with rather longer times, but not greatly longer, when it is necessary to change at Ayr from or into the electric trains that ply between Glasgow and that town. In addition to the Glasgow services there are also others originating at Kilmarnock, Newcastle-on-Tyne or Ayr, or returning thereto. The Newcastle service is a little faster than before its discontinuation in 1973, taking rather more than five hours each way.

The Super Sprinters do not have any first class accommodation and, one is tempted to say, do not need any. The carefully-designed seats are as comfortable as one could wish, and although not all are placed beside a window only a few fail to allow a good view of the lineside. Floors are carpeted. Ventilation is from downwardly-hinged lights above large windows. Tables are narrower towards their inner ends to allow easy entry and exit, a boon for the more portly passenger. Those seats which do not face tables have hinged let-down ledges on the backs of the seats in front of them, on which to stand food and drink. The most noticeable innovation is the spacious push-button-operated toilet compartment, one to each pair of cars, whose door opens, shuts and locks through pressure on small rubber pads. One possible fault in their design is the placing of the alarm handle near the flushing lever. More than once, in my own experience of Sprinter travel on the West Highland line, the train has been brought to a halt between stations by passengers confusing the two.

On most of these trains the provision of refreshments has now returned for all or part of the journey. A youthful attendant from time to time wheels a trolley down the gangway, offering beverages hot and cold, soft or hard, as well as sandwiches, chocolate bars, sweets and potato crisps. Towards the end of each journey a final visit is paid with a plastic bag to collect all the debris. While one may sigh for the restaurant service of the 1930s, when for a price one could eat in style in an elaborately-ornamented ex-L&NWR dining car, the present arrangement probably suits most passengers.

A slight change to the service-pattern, allied to a considerable change in the pattern of connecting boat links to Northern Ireland, has occurred at the time of writing. An early through Sprinter service, leaving Glasgow at 7.30 am in advance of the usual morning train at 8.23, is booked to connect with the new Seacat catamaran service from Stranraer to Belfast, giving an arrival at Donegall Quay, Belfast, at 11.45 am. In the other direction one can leave by Seacat at 4.30 pm and arrive at Glasgow at 9.02 pm. On the face of it, this restores to the business man the ability to leave Glasgow early, do four hours' business or more at Belfast and return to his home the same evening. Whether this will tempt anyone to go the somewhat cheaper way by train and fast boat instead of flying remains to be seen. In the opinion of many Stranraer people, the port is now over-provided with services to Ulster and one will eventually have to be discontinued.

Looking ahead, one can only hope that the Girvan–Stranraer line will survive whatever vicissitudes the immediate future may hold and under whatever form of organisation the British railway system may presently assume. It is still the only rail link with the short sea route to Northern Ireland, and with the large number of sailings from Stranraer every train is in effect a boat train – though the wait at the port can sometimes be very long. One cannot but lament the disappearance of the former facility of being able to take the last evening train from Glasgow to Stranraer and then sleep on the boat which left for Larne at 7 am, since the latter no longer has a long turn-round at Stranraer pier, the vessels being used more intensively, so that no berths are now available on board. In other respects things are as good or better than before, at any rate for the standard class passenger.

The line is certainly being run more economically than before. In the days of steam each train had a crew of three; two now suffice. Fuel costs are lower than would have been the case if all trains were locomotive-hauled, since a two-car Sprinter is less than half the weight of a locomotive hauling three corridor coaches, the equivalent in passenger accommodation. With the closure of stations their maintenance and the wages of the staff no longer add to the annual bill. Possibly the future will see further economies. If the radio-signalling system now successfully operating on the West Highland Line north of Craigendoran Junction were introduced, this would remove the need for visible signalling altogether. On the other side of the equation, it might be possible to attract more passengers by opening some unstaffed halts; Pinwherry seems a possible candidate, and also New Luce, which lies on the track of the Southern Upland Way, walkers along which would then be able to reach a bed at Stranraer or Girvan.

One considerable problem affects the line's future – that of expensive maintenance – in particular of the large fixed structures such as bridges and viaducts. Over many of these there are now severe speed restrictions, and one recalls that one reason advanced by BR for closing the Settle and Carlisle railway (which happily did not happen) was the similar case of the Ribblehead viaduct, because of the huge cost of repairing its crumbling structure. Privatisation of parts or the whole of the British railway system seems now almost certain, but one doubts whether a private purchaser would be forthcoming for a line whose plant was deteriorating and needed extensive renewal. Closure seems much more probable. Remembering the chequered history of the G&PJR in its early days, and bearing in mind the present difficulties, one is disposed to echo the words of Robert Burns:

> But och! I backward cast my eye
>   On prospects drear,
> And forward though I canna see,
>   I guess an' fear.

One is sorry to end on a pessimistic note and hopes to be proved wrong. Stranraer station not so long ago was renovated and given a face-lift, which suggests some optimism on the part of its owners; may it prove not to have been misplaced.

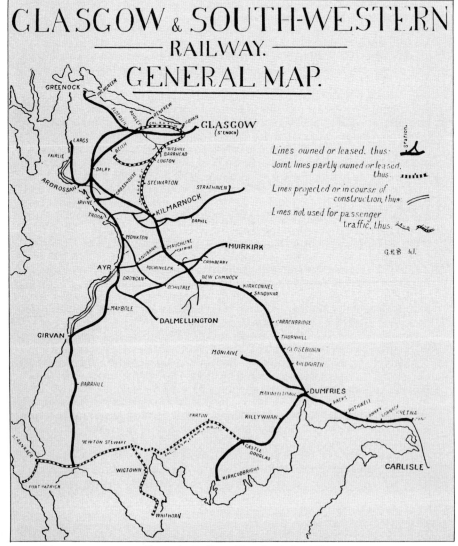

From the Railway Year Book for 1905

Appendix One

Principal Events on the Girvan and Portpatrick Junction Railway

July 1865.	Construction authorised by Act of Parliament.
1872.	Construction commenced.
October 1877.	First train services began on completed line.
July 1879.	Railway put under management of Judicial Factor.
February 1882.	Permission to proceed beyond Challoch Junction denied to G&PJR trains by the PR.
August 1883.	Ban on G&PJR trains beyond Challoch Junction lifted.
August 1887.	Sale of line to new owners and change of title to Ayrshire & Wigtownshire Railway.
February 1892.	Sale of A&WR to G&SWR.
February 1895.	Severe snowstorm disrupts rail services.
1899.	First appearance of corridor stock on boat trains.
December 1908.	Severe snowstorm disrupts rail services.
1914.	First 'peak' year of Girvan–Stranraer services.
1917–1918.	'Trough' years of wartime Girvan–Stranraer services.
January 1923.	Ownership of line passes to LMS Company.
1926.	Restaurant cars first introduced between Glasgow and Stranraer.
June 1927.	First Sunday Excursion train from Glasgow to Portpatrick and back.
1932.	Named trains first run on Glasgow–Stranraer service.
March 1939.	Former turntable at Stranraer replaced by 60 ft table, enabled use of 4–6–0s.
September 1939.	Reduced wartime service begins.
March 1947.	Severe snowstorm disrupts rail services.
January 1948.	Ownership of line passes to British Railways.
November 1959.	Introduction of DMUs on Glasgow–Stranraer service.
June 1965.	Closure of Dumfries–Challoch Junction line shifts all Stranraer-bound trains to Girvan–Stranraer line, including through trains from the South.
	Closure of Pinmore, Pinwherry, Glenwhilly, New Luce, Dunragit, Castle Kennedy and Stranraer Town stations.
May 1980.	Introduction of first through daytime train between London (Euston) and Stranraer named The Northern Irishman.
1984–1987.	Reversion of Glasgow–Stranraer service to locomotive haulage.
October 1988.	Introduction of Super-Sprinter service.

Appendix Two
Selected Timetables: Girvan–Stranraer: 1880–1992

1880.	The service as first established by the G&SWR, which ran the trains with its own locomotives and rolling stock. All trains ran through to and from Glasgow.
1882 to 1883.	The reduced service, operated by a single locomotive and rake of coaches, between Girvan and New Luce. Between New Luce and Stranraer passengers used a special horse-drawn coach service.
1890.	The service offered by the Ayrshire & Wigtownshire Railway, using its own locomotives and rolling stock, from Girvan Old Station, the original southward terminus of the G&SWR; here connections were made from and to Glasgow.
1900.	Now owned by the G&SWR, the line offers a somewhat faster and more frequent service of through trains from and to Glasgow.
1910.	The service at the end of the Edwardian era, more frequent than before, with a fast mid-day northbound service and the famous 'Paddy' offering a journey time of under 2½ hours to Glasgow in the late evening.
1918.	The nadir following the Edwardian zenith – fewer trains daily even than in 1880, on slower timings.
1923.	Under LMS control things are beginning to look up again, with more frequent services although no great improvement in speed. The 'Paddy' has now re-appeared, though on a much slower timing.
1931.	Service-frequency has again increased, with extra week-end trains, including one on Sunday. No marked accelerations yet.
1939.	The peak of achievement just before the Second World War. Note the numbers of boat trains, the extent of the Sunday service and the accelerated 'Paddy', now named *The Irishman*.
1940.	The trough following the second peak – with, however, quite respectable timings for the stopping trains, now mostly hauled by 4–6–0s.
1948.	The service in the first year of British Railways' management. Week-end trains have re-appeared, and the 'Paddy' has quite a fast timing.
1961.	The service is much as before. The whole service, however, is now DMU operated and a little faster in consequence.
1968.	The service in the first year after the abolition of steam traction. DMUs operate the Glasgow services, which no longer use the now-dismantled St Enoch station. Trains to or from places across the Border are locomotive-hauled. South of Girvan all stations are closed except Barrhill. The night sleeper from and to Euston now uses this route.
1980.	In this year service-frequency between Girvan and Stranraer reached its height, with both day and night through trains to and from Euston.
1988.	Locomotive-hauled trains have temporarily replaced the now time-expired DMUs. The through trains to London still run but this is their final year.
1992.	The full Super-Sprinter service at the time of writing, with record 51-minute timings from Stranraer to Girvan.

Selected Timetables; Girvan-Stranraer: 1880 to Present Day:

1880

Glasgow St Enoch	6.45	8.15	11.15	4.15
Girvan	8.41	10.45	1.46	6.34
Pinmore		10.58	1.59	6.47
Pinwherry	8.58	11.07	2.07	6.55
Barrhill		11.18	2.17	7.06
Glenwhilly		11.35	2.33	7.23
New Luce		11.50	2.43	7.33
Dunragit	9.39	12.05	3.07	7.48
Castle Kennedy		12.12	3.15	7.55
Stranraer Town		12.18	3.22	8.00
Stranraer Harbour	9.53			

Stranraer Harbour	8.15			
Stranraer Town	7.10	11.20	4.20	
Castle Kennedy	7.16	11.27	4.27	8.21
Dunragit	7.23	11.35	4.35	8.28
New Luce	7.38	11.49	4.49	
Glenwhilly	7.48	11.58	4.58	
Barrhill	8.03	12.12	5.12	
Pinwherry	8.12	12.21	5.21	9.09
Pinmore	8.20	12.29	5.29	
Girvan	8.30	12.39	5.39	9.26
Glasgow St Enoch	11.25	3.28	8.30	11.25

February 1882-August 1882

Glasgow St Enoch	6.45	4.15
Girvan	10.00	6.34
Pinmore	10.14	6.47
Pinwherry	10.22	6.55
Barrhill	10.30	7.03
Glenwhilly	10.46	7.19
New Luce	10.55	7.30
Dunragit	Road coach	
Castle Kennedy	service	
Stranraer Town	12.15	8.50

Stranraer Town	6.30	3.30
Castle Kennedy	Road coach	
Dunragit	service	
New Luce	7.45	4.50
Glenwhilly	7.55	5.02
Barrhill	8.11	5.20
Pinwherry	8.19	5.29
Pinmore	8.27	5.38
Girvan	8.40	5.50
Glasgow St Enoch	11.22	8.45

1890

Glasgow St Enoch	5.50	8.15	11.30	4.15
Girvan (Old Stn.)	7.50	10.38	2.05	6.25
Pinmore	8.05	10.53	2.22	6.40
Pinwherry	8.15	11.03	2.32	6.50
Barrhill	8.25	11.13	2.42	7.00
Glenwhilly	8.42	11.30	2.59	7.17
New Luce	8.52	11.40	3.09	7.27
Dunragit	9.06	11.56	3.25	7.41
Castle Kennedy	9.13	12.03	3.32	7.49
Stranraer Town	9.20	12.10	3.40	7.55

Stranraer Harbour				8.25
Stranraer Town	7.10	11.30	4.15	
Castle Kennedy	7 18	11.36	4.22	
Dunragit	7.26	11.50	4.30	8.33
New Luce	7.40		4.44	
Glenwhilly	7.50		4.54	
Barrhill	8.07	12.22	5.10	9.08
Pinwherry	8.17	12.30	5.20	9.15
Pinmore	8.27		5.30	
Girvan (Old Stn.)	8.45	12.50	5.45	9.35
Glasgow St. Enoch	11.27	3.30	8.30	11.45

1900

Station					SO	
Glasgow St .Enoch	5.15	8.40	12.30	2.07	4.15	5.00
Girvan	7.55	10.35	2.15	4.00	6.25	6.50
Pinmore	8.07	10.47	2.27		6.35	
Pinwherry	8.21	10.56	2.37	4.14	6.45	7.07
Barrhill	8.31	11.06	2.47	4.24	6.55	
Glenwhilly	8.46	11.22	3.03		7.11	
New Luce	8.56	11.34	3.13		7.21	
Dunragit	9.09	11.47	3.26	4.55	7.35	7.45
Castle Kennedy	9.16	11.55	3.33		7.42	
Stranraer Town	9.21	12.00	3.38	5.05	7.47	
Stranraer Harbour						8.00

Station	MO					
Stranraer Harbour				12.35		8.30
Stranraer Town	6.15	7.20	11.00		4.15	
Castle Kennedy		7.27	11.07		4.22	
Dunragit	6.26	7.35	11.17	12.47	4.30	8.42
New Luce		7.48	11.34		4.44	
Glenwhilly		7.58	11.45		4.54	
Barrhill	6.56	8.12	12.01		5.09	9.13
Pinwherry	7.05	8.23	12.11	1.22	5.19	9.22
Pinmore		8.33	12.21		5.29	
Girvan	7.20	8.45	12.31	1.37	5.39	9.37
Glasgow St. Enoch	9.08	10.40	2.22	3.35	7.27	11.35

1910

	SO					
Glasgow St Enoch	5.10	8.40	12.30	2.07	4.10	5.10
Girvan	7.40	10.35	2.13	3.55	6.00	6.50
Pinmore	7.52	10.47	2.25			7.00
Pinwherry	8.03	10.56	2.36	4.10	6.17	7.10
Barrhill	8.16	11.06	2.47	4.20		7.20
Glenwhilly	8.31	11.21	3.03			7.36
New Luce	8.41	11.30	3.13	4.41		7.46
Dunragit	8.54	11.43	3.26	4.54	6.55	8.00
Castle Kennedy	9.01	11.52	3.33			8.07
Stranraer Town	9.06	12.00	3.38	5.05		8.15
Stranraer Harbour					7.10	

	MO					
Stranraer Harbour	6.05			12.50		9.55
Stranraer Town		7.20	11.30		4.15	
Castle Kennedy		7.27	11.37		4.22	
Dunragit	6.16	7.35	11.49	1.02	4.30	
New Luce		7.48	12.03		4.44	
Glenwhilly		7.58	12.13		4.54	
Barrhill	6.46	8.15	12.29		5.08	
Pinwherry	6.54	8.25	12.40		5.19	
Pinmore	7.04	8.35	12.50		5.29	
Girvan	7.14	8.45	1.00	1.50	5.39	10.50 (pass)
Glasgow St Enoch	9.05	10.40	2.55	3.45	7.31	12.20

1918

Glasgow St Enoch	8.40	11.00	4.10
Girvan	11.05	1.20	6.45
Pinmore	11.20	1.35	7.00
Pinwherry	11.30	1.43	7.08
Barrhill	11.42	1.54	7.18
Glenwhilly	11.58	2.10	7.34
New Luce	12.08	2.20	7.44
Dunragit	12.22	2.35	7.58
Castle Kennedy	12.29	2.45	8.06
Stranraer Town	12.35	2.50	8.15

Stranraer Town	6.30	10.10	4.00
Castle Kennedy	6.38	10.17	4.07
Dunragit	6.47	10.37	4.15
New Luce	7.03	10.53	4.28
Glenwhilly	7.15	11.05	4.39
Barrhill	7.31	11.21	4.55
Pinwherry	7.45	11.33	5.05
Pinmore	7.54	11.43	5.15
Girvan	8.03	11.55	5.25
Glasgow St Enoch	10.15	2.13	7.48

1923

Glasgow St Enoch	5.00	9.00	12.30	4.10	5.55
Girvan	7.50	10.42	2.13	6.03	7.55
Pinmore	8.05	10.57	2.28	6.18	
Pinwherry	8.15	11.05	2.36	6.26	8.15
Barrhill	8.25	11.15	2.47	6.36	8.23
Glenwhilly	8.40	11.30	3.03	6.52	
New Luce	8.48	11.38	3.13	7.02	8.47
Dunragit	9.00	11.50	3.26	7.15	9.00
Castle Kennedy	9.07	11.57	3.33		9.07
Stranraer Town	9.15	12.05	3.38		
Stranraer Harbour				7.28	9.15

Stranraer Harbour			9.25	
Stranraer Town	7.00	11.32	4.10	
Castle Kennedy	7.07	11.39	4.17	
Dunragit	7.15	11.50	4.25	
New Luce	7.31	12.05	4.38	
Glenwhilly	7.43	12.17	4.50	
Barrhill	7.59	12.33	5.06	
Pinwherry	8.12	12.43	5.15	
Pinmore	8.22	12.54	5.25	
Girvan	8.33	1.04	5.40	10.35
Glasgow St Enoch	10.24	3.02	7.38	12.05

1931

			FO				SX	SO
Glasgow St Enoch	5.10	9.00	10.17	12.30	3.55	5.10	8.00	8.00
Girvan	7.50	10.45	12.03	2.16	5.43	6.50	9.43	9.43
Pinmore	8.05	11.03		2.31		7.07		9.58
Pinwherry	8.12	11.08		2.39	6.01	7.15		10.04
Barrhill	8.23	11.18		2.50		7.26		10.13
Glenwhilly	8.38	11.33		3.05		7.41		
New Luce	8.46	11.41		3.13		7.50		10.39
Dunragit	8.58	11.52		3.24	6.42	8.02		10.52
Castle Kennedy	9.06	12.00		3.32	6.50	8.08		
Stranraer Town	9.13	12.08		3.38		8.16		
Stranraer Harbour			1.16		6.58		10.57	11.05

			FO				SuO
Stranraer Harbour			12.30		5.15		9.27	
Stranraer Town	7.05	11.40		4.05		7.20		6.20
Castle Kennedy	7.12	11.47		4.12				
Dunragit	7.19	11.53	12.42	4.18		7.33		
New Luce	7.33	12.07		4.33		7.50		
Glenwhilly	7.45	12.19		4.45				
Barrhill	8.00	12.35		5.00		8.16		
Pinwherry	8.10	12.43		5.08		8.24		
Pinmore	8.22	12.55		5.17				
Girvan	8.32	1.06	1.37	5.26	6.33	8.42	10.38	7.31
Glasgow St Enoch	10.21	2.55	3.28	7.24	8.11	10.23	12.15	9.22

1939

Station		FSO		FSO		SO				*The Irishman*	Sundays pm	pm
Glasgow St Enoch	5.13	8.15	9.00	10.35	12.30	3.15	3.50	5.10	8.05		5.35	8.05
Girvan	7.42	9.48	10.36	12.05	2.04	4.44	5.25	6.39	9.43		7.37	9.46
Pinmore	7.58		10.51		2.19			6.54				
Pinwherry	8.06		10.57		2.25			7.00				
Barrhill	8.20		11.07		2.35			7.10				
Glenwhilly	8.37		11.20		2.50			7.25				
New Luce	8.45		11.30		2.59			7.34				
Dunragit	8.56		11.39		3.09		6.19	7.47				
Castle Kennedy	9.03		11.46		3.16			7.54				
Stranraer Town	9.09		11.54		3.22			8.00				
Stranraer Harbour		10.58		1.18		6.00	6.30		10.57		9.19	11.00

Station		FSO				FSO				*The Irishman*	Sundays pm	pm
Stranraer Harbour		10.40		12.50		5.25		9.17			7.30	8.25
Stranraer Town	7.25		11.40		4.08		7.13					
Castle Kennedy	7.31		11.48		4.14							
Dunragit	7.38	10.55	11.55	1.03	4.19		7.23					
New Luce	7.52		12.08		4.32		7.41					
Glenwhilly	8.04		12.20		4.43		7.51					
Barrhill	8.19		12.36		4.58		8.06					
Pinwherry	8.28		12.46		5.05		8.13					
Pinmore	8.37		12.57		5.14							
Girvan	8.46	12.01	1.06	1.56	5.23	6.39	8.30	10.20			8.34	9.31
Glasgow St Enoch	10.20	1.35	2.40	3.28	7.04	8.12	10.17	11.50			10.24	11.23

1940

Glasgow St Enoch	8.45	12.30	5.10	8.05
Girvan	10.27	2.13	6.40	9.46
Pinmore	10.42	2.27	6.55	
Pinwherry	10.48	2.33	7.01	
Barrhill	10.58	2.43	7.11	
Glenwhilly	11.13	2.58	7.26	
New Luce	11.21	3.06	7.34	
Dunragit	11.33	3.18	7.46	
Castle Kennedy	11.39	3.24	7.52	
Stranraer Town	11.45	3.30	7.58	
Stranraer Harbour				11.01

Stranraer Harbour				9.17
Stranraer Town	7.05	11.55	4.20	
Castle Kennedy	7.10	12.00	4.26	
Dunragit	7.17	12.06	4.31	
New Luce	7.30	12.18	4.44	
Glenwhilly	7.41	12.28	4.54	
Barrhill	7.54	12.43	5.08	
Pinwherry	8.02	12.51	5.15	
Pinmore	8.10	12.59	5.23	
Girvan	8.20	1.08	5.31	10.25
Glasgow St Enoch	10.01	2.59	7.15	12.00

1948

			FSO			Sundays
Glasgow St Enoch	8.55	12.30	2.50	5.10	8.15	8.15
Girvan	10.44	2.11	4.44	6.50	10.40	9.57
Pinmore	11.01	2.28		7.08		
Pinwherry	11.08	2.35		7.15		
Barrhill	11.19	2.46		7.26		
Glenwhilly	11.34	3.01		7.41		
New Luce	11.42	3.09		7.49		
Dunragit	11.55	3.22		8.01		
Castle Kennedy	12.02	3.29		8.07		
Stranraer Town	12.08	3.35		8.13		
Stranraer Harbour				5.55	11.55	11.08

			FSO			
Stranraer Harbour			12.45		9.30	
Stranraer Town	7.20	11.48		4.20		
Castle Kennedy	7.26	11.54		4.27		
Dunragit	7.32	12.01		4.32		
New Luce	7.45	12.15		4.45		
Glenwhilly	7.57	12.26		4.56		
Barrhill	8.12	12.41		5.11	10.15	
Pinwherry	8.21	12.49		5.18		
Pinmore	8.30	12.57		5.26		
Girvan	8.40	1.08	2.02	5.35	10.30	
Glasgow St Enoch	10.21	3.07	4.06	7.30	12.15	

1961

					SO	SX	Sundays
Glasgow St Enoch							
Girvan	10.40	2.10	4.58	6.42	10.35	10.42	10.28
Pinmore	10.52	2.22		6.54	10.47		
Pinwherry	10.57	2.27		6.59	10.52		
Barrhill	11.07	2.37		7.09	11.02		
Glenwhilly	11.22	2.52		7.24	11.17		
New Luce	11.30	3.00		7.32			
Dunragit	11.40	3.10		7.42	11.37		
Castle Kennedy	11.46	3.16		7.48	11.44		
Stranraer Town	11.52	3.22		7.54			
Stranraer Harbour				6.15	11.50	11.48	11.34

					SO		Sundays
Stranraer Harbour	7.40	11.35			9.15		6.15
Stranraer Town			12.55	4.40			
Castle Kennedy	7.45		1.00	4.45			
Dunragit	7.50		1.05	4.50			
New Luce	8.01		1.16	5.01			
Glenwhilly	8.11		1.26	5.11			
Barrhill	8.26		1.41	5.26	*		6.57
Pinwherry	8.33		1.48	5.33			
Pinmore	8.41		1.56	5.41			
Girvan	8.49	12.37	2.04	5.49	10.20		7.18
Glasgow St Enoch							

* Conditional stop to set down.

1968

Station			SO		SX	FO	SX	Sundays	
Glasgow Central	8.30	11.26		15.30	21.00			9.00	21.05
Paisley	8.41	11.37		15.41	21.11			9.11	21.16
London (Euston)							20.40		
Newcastle-on-Tyne			8.15			23.45			
Carlisle			10.10			1.17	2.32		
Dumfries			10.55			2.00	3.14		
Ayr	9.38	12.14	12.31	16.40	22.05			10.05	22.10
Girvan	10.08	12.44		17.10	22.41		4.59	10.35	22.42
Barrhill	10.32	13.08		17.34	23.05			11.00	23.07
Stranraer	11.12	13.49	14.18	18.14	23.52	5.07	6.10	11.45	23.52

Station		SO				FO		Sundays	
Stranraer	11.30	13.30	14.05	18.30	21.20	21.30	22.10	18.15	19.30
Barrhill	12.14		14.49	19.14	22.04			18.59	20.13
Girvan	12.34		15.09	19.34	22.24			19.18	20.33
Ayr	13.05		15.40	20.05	22.54			19.50	21.05
Dumfries		16.25				00.30	1.05		
Carlisle		17.16				1.13	1.43		
Newcastle-on-Tyne		19.11				2.51			
London (Euston)							7.47		
Paisley	14.00		16.40	21.00	23.36			20.53	21.53
Glasgow Central	14.10		16.50	21.10	23.50			20.53	22.04

1980

Station				SO		SO		SX	Sundays	
Glasgow Central	8.35	11.35		15.30		18.00	22.00	Slpg.	9.00	15.00
Paisley	8.46	11.46						car	9.11	15.11
London (Euston)					10.15			20.55		
Carlisle			12.04		15.07			2.02		
Dumfries			12.53		15.42			2.42		
Ayr	9.50	12.35		16.41	17.09	19.06	23.06		10.09	16.11
Girvan	10.19	13.03		17.09	19.06	19.38	23.35		10.37	16.39
Barrhill	10.44	13.29		17.35		20.02	23.59		11.04	17.02
Stranraer	11.25	14.10	16.01	18.16	18.35	20.44	00.41	6.06	11.47	17.44

Station			SO		SO				SO	Sundays		
Stranraer	7.20	10.35	11.00	13.10	15.05	18.36	21.25	22.00	01.20	13.06	18.06	22.00
Barrhill	7.58	11.13	11.41	13.53	15.43	19.14	22.03		*	13.44	18.44	
Girvan	8.21	11.35	12.02	14.17	16.05	19.36	22.25	23.08		14.06	19.06	23.06
Ayr	8.55	12.09	12.35	14.51	16.39	20.10	23.01	23.55		14.40	19.40	23.42
Dumfries								1.28				1.28
Carlisle		15.15						2.23				2.29
London (Euston)		20.09						7.59				7.25
Paisley	10.07		13.07	15.45	17.39	21.07	23.51		Slpg.	15.39	20.39	
Glasgow Central	10.20		13.20	16.00	17.51	21.20	00.04		car	15.51	20.51	

*7th July to 25th August, from Stranraer Harbour to Blackpool North, arr 07.36

1988

							Sundays	
Glasgow Central	8.23	12.23			21.53	*Slpg.*	8.35	15.37
Paisley	8.34	12.34			22.04	car	8.46	15.48
London (Euston)			9.45			20.20		
Carlisle								
Kilmarnock			16.17					
Ayr	9.20	13.13	16.55	19.28	22.43	4.41	9.30	16.27
Girvan	9.49	13.44	17.25	19.59	23.14	5.09	10.01	16.55
Barrhill	10.11	14.07	17.51	20.25	23.37		10.28	17.18
Stranraer	10.46	14.46	18.29	21.05	00.19	6.16	11.07	17.53

							Sundays		
Stranraer	7.00	10.55	14.25	18.35	21.15	22.35	14.25	18.35	22.25
Barrhill	7.33	11.33	14.58	19.08	21.53		15.03	19.08	
Girvan	7.56	11.57	15.21	19.31	22.18	23.21	15.28	19.31	23.21
Ayr	8.27	12.31	15.52	20.07	22.49	23.50	16.02	20.07	23.50
Kilmarnock		12.55							
Carlisle		14.41							
London (Euston)		19.24				7.55			
Paisley	9.00		16.29	20.42		*Slpg.*	16.41	20.42	
Glasgow Central	9.12		16.43	20.54		car	16.53	20.54	

1992

							Sundays		
Glasgow Central		8.13	11.53			22.23	8.48	12.57	15.37
Paisley		8.24	12.04			22.34	8.59	13.08	15.48
Newcastle-on-Tyne				12.38					
Carlisle				14.10					
Kilmarnock	7.50			15.45					
Ayr	8.20	9.00	12.40	16.15	19.30	23.13	9.37	13.50	16.28
Girvan	8.48	9.28	13.08	16.41	20.01	23.39	10.03	14.16	16.59
Barrhill	9.08	9.48	13.28	17.01	20.21	23.59	10.23	14.36	17.19
Stranraer	9.43	10.23	14.04	17.38	20.56	00.34	11.00	15.20	17.54

							Sundays		
Stranraer	7.03	10.00	11.00	14.30	18.48	21.25	11.00	14.30	18.30
Barrhill	7.37	10.38	11.33	15.06	19.22	21.49	11.34	15.06	19.04
Girvan	7.54	10.56	11.51	15.23	19.39	22.06	11.51	15.23	19.24
Ayr	8.27	11.24	12.24	15.56	20.12	22.40	12.24	15.56	19.57
Kilmarnock			12.47						
Carlisle			14.21						
Newcastle-on-Tyne			15.51						
Paisley	8.59			16.32	20.52	23.15	12.59	16.32	20.35
Glasgow Central	9.11			16.45	21.03	23.28	13.18	16.47	20.47

Appendix Three

Types and Classes of Steam Locomotives used between Girvan and Stranraer

Listed in order of construction

Class	Type	Designer	Date of first building
G&SW '141' class	0-4-2	P. Stirling	1866
G&SW '8' class	2-4-0	J. Stirling	1870
G&SW '221' class	0-4-2	J. Stirling	1875
G&SW '13' class	0-6-0	J. Stirling	1877
G&SW '157' class	2-4-0	H. Smellie	1879
G&SW '119' class	4-4-0	H. Smellie	1882
G&SW '22' class	0-6-0	H. Smellie	1886
	0-6-0	Unknown	1886 1
G&SW '8' class	4-4-0	J. Manson	1892
G&SW '306' class	4-4-0	J. Manson	1895
G&SW '279' class	0-6-0	P. Drummond	1913
G&SW '131' class	4-4-0	P. Drummond	1913
G&SW '137' class	4-4-0	P. Drummond	1915
G&SW '403' class	2-6-0	P. Drummond	1915
HR 'River' class	4-6-0	F.G. Smith	1915 2
CR '60' class	4-6-0	W. Pickersgill	1916
LMS class '4P'	4-4-0	H. Fowler	1924 3
LMS class '5MT'	2-6-0	G. Hughes, modified by H. Fowler	1926
LMS class '5X'	4-6-0	H. Fowler	1930 4
LMS class '5X'	4-6-0	W.A. Stanier	1934 5
LMS class '5MT'	4-6-0	W.A. Stanier	1934
BR class '5'	4-6-0	R.A. Riddles	1951
BR class '7'	4-6-2	R.A. Riddles	1951
BR class '6'	4-6-2	R.A. Riddles	1952

1 Built for the Ayrshire & Wigtownshire Railway and used during 1886/92.
2 Originally built for the HR but sold later to the CR.
3 3-cylinder 'Midland Compounds'.
4 'Baby Scots' (otherwise known as 'Patriots').
5 'Jubilees'.

Index

Accidents to passenger trains:
  1895 46
  1908 46
  1947 47
  to freight trains:
  1922 48
  1928 49
Acts of Parliament
  1865 6
  1870 7
  1874 8
  1883 10
  1886 11
  1892 20

Barrhill, sation/village 6, 17, 19, 23, 28, 34,
  40, 46, 49, 51, 55−6
Beeching Report 6, 20, 55
Blair, J. 12
Bouch, Sir Thomas 9
Bryson tablet catcher 15, 19
Buffet car services 20, 35, 56

Cairnryan Port 18−9
Castle Kennedy station 19, 30
Challoch Junction 8−10, 12, 19, 21, 31, 36, 52
Chirmorie summit 21, 28, 40, 46, 51
Closure of PR metals to G&PJR 10

Drummond, P., Loco. Supt, G&SWR 38
Dunragit, station/signal box 17, 19, 28, 31

'Fast Belfast' 33
Fowler, Sir H., CME, LMS 42

Glendoune bank & cutting 19, 21, 51
Glenwhilly, station/signal box 17, 19, 28,
  47−8, 51, 56

Haldane, J. 8
Hughes, G., CME, L&YR & LMS 42
Hutchinson, Genl. BOT Inspector 8

'Irishman' 33

Locomotives
  Ex-NLR tanks 32, 36−7
  A&WR 0−6−0s 32, 37, 46
  P. Stirling 0−4−2, G&SWR 36
  J. Stirling, various, G&SWR 36
  H. Smellie 2−4−0, G&SWR 36
  H. Smellie 'Wee Bogies', G&SWR 37
  J. Manson, '8' class 4−4−0, G&SWR 38
  J. Manson 'Greenock Bogies', G&SWR 38
  P. Drummond '131' & '137' class 4−4−0,
    G&SWR 38−40
  P. Drummond 0−6−0 'Pumpers' 39, 50
  P. Drummond 2−6−0 G&SWR 40
  'Midland Compound' 4−4−0 40, 52
  Fowler '2,P' 4−4−0 41
  Hughes 2−6−0, LMS 41, 51
  Pickersgill 4−6−0 class '60' 42
  Stanier 'Black Five' 4−6−0 43
  Stanier 'Jubilee' 5XP 4−6−0 43, 47, 52
  Fowler 'Baby Scot' 4−6−0 44
  ex-HR 'River' 4−6−0 44, 52
  BR standard class '5' 4−6−0 44−5
  BR standard class '6' 4−6−2 45, 56

BR standard class '7' 4−6−2 45, 56
BR diesel-electric class '27', '37', '47' 57

Manson, James, Loco. Supt., G&SWR 13, 15,
  32, 37, 39
Maps of G&PJR 4, 14
Multiple-unit diesel trains 20, 34−5, 57

New Luce station/signal box 10, 17, 19, 28,
  31, 36, 47, 51−4, 59
'Northern Irishman' 56

'Paddy' evening boat train 14, 32−4, 38
Pickersgill, W., Loco. Supt., CR 42
Pilling, Abraham, railway builder 8
Pinmore station/signal box 19, 23, 31, 46, 49,
  51−3
Pinwherry station/signal box 8, 17, 19, 23, 31,
  46, 49−50, 52−3, 59
Portpatrick 7, 20, 33
Pullman restaurant cars 35

Railway companies (actual & projected)
  Ayrshire & Wigtownshire 11−4, 37
  Caledonian 10−1, 17, 35
  Glasgow & Belfast Union 7
  Glasgow, Kilmarnock, Paisley & Ayr 7
  Great North of Scotland 5
  Glasgow, Stranraer & Northern Ireland 7
  Highland 5, 21, 38
  London Midland & Scottish 16−7, 20,
    33−4, 39
  London & North Eastern 19
  London & North Western 11, 19, 35, 39
  Midland 11, 39
  Portpatrick Rly. 7−11, 28
  Portpatrick & Wigtownshire Joint Committee
    11
  Wigtownshire 11
Restaurant cars 18, 33−5

Sabbath observance 33
Salisbury disaster of 1906 15, 32
Seacat catamaran service, Stranraer−Belfast
  59
Sealink Ferries 57
Sleeping car trains 45, 55
Smellie, H., Loco. Supt., G&SWR 37
Smillie, Bob 51−4
Smith, David L. 14, 33, 39, 41−4, 49−50,
  51−4
Smith, F.G., Loco. Supt., HR 44
Snowstorms holding up trains 46
Southern Upland Way 59
Stanier, Sir W.A., CME, LMS 43
Sunday excursions to Portpatrick 17, 33
Super-Sprinter services 21, 57−8
'Swan's Neck' 28, 48

Viaducts
  Daltangan 23
  Kinclaer 23
  Lagansarroch 23
  Lig Burn 23
  Stinchar 8

World War I 6, 16, 33
World War II 6, 17, 19, 33